THE
BIRTH
ORDER
EFFECT
for Couples

THE
BIRTH
ORDER
EFFECT
for Couples

How Birth Order Affects
Your Relationships — and What
You Can Do About It

CLIFF ISAACSON
with MEG SCHNEIDER

FAIR WINDS
PRESS
GLOUCESTER, MASSACHUSETTS

First published in the USA in 2004 by
Fair Winds Press
33 Commercial Street
Gloucester, MA 01930

Library of Congress Cataloging-in-Publication Data

Isaacson, Clifford E., 1934–
  Birth order effect for couples : how birth order affects your relationships and what you can do about it / Cliff Isaacson and Meg Schneider.
      p. cm.
   ISBN 1-59233-023-1
  1. Man-woman relationships. 2. Birth order. 3. Parent and child. I. Schneider, Meg F. II. Title.
   HQ801.I75 2004
   306.7--dc22

                                        2003018296

10 9 8 7 6 5 4 3 2 1

Cover design by Stefan Killen Design
Book design by Stefan Killen Design

Printed and bound in Canada

For our spouses, Kathy and Bud

The journey is the reward

Table of Contents

Introduction 9
  What Is the Birth Order Effect?
Chapter One 13
  What's Your Birth Order?
Chapter Two 29
  The Birth Order Effect and Relationships
Chapter Three 45
  The Only Child
Chapter Four 67
  The First Born
Chapter Five 85
  The Second Born
Chapter Six 107
  The Third Born
Chapter Seven 123
  The Fourth Born
Chapter Eight 141
  The Birth Order Effect and Communication
Chapter Nine 157
  The Birth Order Effect and Conflict Resolution
Chapter Ten 173
  Putting the Birth Order Effect to Work for You
Acknowledgments 191
About the Authors 192

What Is the Birth Order Effect?

M any of us are familiar with the concept of birth order—that is, the concept that was developed by Alfred Adler nearly a century ago. In his 1918 book, *Understanding Human Nature*, Adler theorized that a child's personality is shaped largely by his or her chronological place in the family, because parents tend to treat children differently according to the order of their birth. He identified four birth-order personalities—the only child, the oldest child, the middle child, and the youngest child—and attached personality traits to thesechronological positions in the family. For example, under Adler's birth order, the oldest child is a natural leader, the youngest child is spoiled, and the middle child is continually struggling to get some parental attention.

I read Adler's book in 1969, and the concept of understanding human beings through birth order seemed to me to hold much promise. I pursued the subject, reading Walter Toman's *The Family Constellation* and Lucille Forer's *The Birth Order Factor*. Unfortunately, my hopes of gaining valuable insights into human nature through birth order were not realized. The more I examined the subject, the more convinced I became that birth order was too vague to be of much use.

Then I ran across a paper by Taibi Kahler, a prominent researcher in Transactional Analysis, in which he described five patterns of behavior. It seemed to me that these behavior patterns, or "mini scripts" in Transactional Analysis terms, could be related to birth order. The "mini scripts" are messages that drive our behavior: Hurry up; Please me; Be perfect; Be strong; and Try hard. I compared these messages and Kahler's descriptions to the personalities of my five children, and I found that each one of our children fit one of the behavior patterns he described. Then I began to ask people I was counseling about their birth orders; by comparing my clients' personalities with my children's personalities, I discovered that Kahler had identified a pattern that was related to birth order. Since then, I have confirmed this birth order concept in more than 30,000 counseling sessions with about 6,000 clients. My clients are the ones who have taught me about the Birth Order Effect, how it functions, and how to deal with it.

The true complexities of birth order go far beyond Adler's concepts, which are insufficient to describe many of us. Some of us have older or younger siblings, yet seem to have the personalities of "only children." Others don't fit into any of the Adlerian birth-order places. And, contrary to Adler's theories about parent-child interaction, I have found that many of my clients' difficulties stem not from their relationships with their parents but from early experiences with their brothers and sisters. The coping strategies we developed in childhood to deal with our siblings, I discovered, are the same ones we use in adulthood to deal with our spouses, our friends, our children, and even our business colleagues.

The five birth order personalities I have identified are Only Child, First Born, Second Born, Third Born, and Fourth Born. Each of these places in the family comes with its own set of challenges to meet, and each Birth Order Personality develops its own way of coping with those challenges. Our birth order personalities are established as early as age two, and, once set, those personalities are ours for life.

In most cases (but certainly not always), our birth order personalities correspond to our chronological place in the family, and birth order personalities will proceed in order from the oldest to the youngest child. For example, if the oldest child of three is a First Born personality, the next child will be a Second Born and the youngest will be a Third Born. If the oldest child develops a Second Born personality, the next child will be a Third Born and the youngest will be a Fourth Born. Even twins organize themselves into consecutive birth order personalities: If the oldest child is a First Born, the twins will be a Second Born and a Third Born.

The child following a Second Born by as many as fourteen years still can be a Third Born. The child following a Third Born by as many as ten years can still be a Fourth Born. The child following a Fourth Born will be an Only Child personality.

It is possible to have an entire family of Only Child personalities. More commonly, birth order repeats itself in large families. For example, in a family of eight children where the oldest child is a Fourth Born, the fifth child will also be a Fourth Born. Once started, birth order will progress in numerical order. I never have found a progression of First Born, Third Born, Second Born, Fourth Born. Therefore, if the Birth Order Personality of one sibling is identified, the others can be identified: If the middle child in a family of five is a Third Born, the next oldest will be a Second Born and the next youngest will be a Fourth Born.

There are exceptions to the correlation between chrono-logical place in the family and Birth Order Personality. People with older or younger siblings can have Only Child personalities if there is a difference of five or more years between siblings, or if their parents had help when the younger child was born so that the older child didn't experience a loss of love to the baby. The child born after a Fourth Born will be an Only regardless of age difference between the two, but this Only can become a First Born if another child is born.

A child who dies may or may not count in the birth order progression, depending on circumstances. I have run across a few oldest children who were Second Born personalities because of a baby born before them, even though the older sibling died before they were born.

Sometimes a mother under stress can determine the birth order of her oldest or youngest child. Stress causes birth order characteristics to become more pronounced, so this child develops his or her personality to cope with Mom rather than with siblings. In this situation, daughters will develop the Birth Order Personality immediately following that of Mom's, while sons will develop the same Birth Order Personality as Mom's. For example, a Second Born mother would cause her daughter to become a Third Born; her son would be a Second Born. The most common scenario I have seen is a Third Born mother causing her oldest child to become a Fourth Born daughter or a Third Born son. First Born mothers seem to have the least impact on their child's Birth Order Personality, while Only Child mothers tend to reinforce the Only Child characteristics of their eldest children.

Because of these exceptions, the birth order descriptions and quizzes at the end of the first chapter are more useful than mere chronology to identify one's true Birth Order Personality.

Thanks to my clients, who give me more information when I need it, correct me when I'm wrong, and affirm my judgment when I'm right, I am always learning more about the Birth Order Effect. I hope you will enjoy this journey of discovery as much as I do.

CHAPTER ONE

What's Your
Birth Order?

Bill and Bonnie had a fairy tale romance. They met by chance in a bar one night and fell to talking. The attraction was instantaneous and mutual. They felt as though they were soul mates; they had similar likes and dislikes, similar opinions, similar interests. They were so comfortable with each other that they moved in together within three weeks of their first meeting, well on their way to their own version of "happily ever after."

Bonnie had some loose ends to tie up; she had left her previous husband three months before she met Bill, and she was in the process of formalizing the divorce. Still, there was no doubt in either's mind that they wanted to be together forever, and they eased effortlessly into a daily routine of work, domestic chores and the occasional night out at a bar or nightclub. After two years, Bonnie's divorce was final, and she and Bill got married. About a year later, they had a baby, and their daily routine concentrated almost exclusively on work and domestic chores. The nights out stopped. They were settling down now that they were parents.

Then one day, four years after they met and two years after they were married, Bonnie announced she wanted a divorce.

Does this tale sound familiar? It should. According to a study by the Centers for Disease Control and Prevention, one of every five first marriages ends in divorce within five years. After ten years, that figure rises to one in three. The same study showed that second marriages end in divorce or separation at even higher rates than first marriages— twenty-three percent of second marriages end within five years, and almost two of every five end after ten years.

That's the bad news. The good news is that, for the first time, there is a new tool to help us understand why a couple has conflict, the roots of the conflict and, most important, how to resolve the conflict. This new tool is the Birth Order Effect. Once you understand what the Birth Order Effect is and how it influences your relationship, the troubles in your relationship will diminish significantly, and your odds of achieving "happily ever after" go up proportionally.

Here's how understanding birth order will help you:

It's going to help you clean up the chaos in your relationship. Insight will replace frustration as you come to understand yourself and your spouse. You'll learn why your relationship works the way it does.

It's going to add satisfaction to your relationship that you didn't know was possible. You won't have to walk around on eggshells for fear of offending your partner; love will be something you experience rather than a goal to be achieved. You'll know what to say, how to interpret your partner, and what will please him or her.

It's going to fill in the details of your relationship so it makes sense to you. Feelings will become understandable; you'll discover that your partner really does care about how you feel. You'll be able to tell the difference between positive and negative communication, and a whole new world of feelings will open up to you.

It's going to make your relationship safer, more comfortable and more enjoyable. If you have been carrying the bulk of the relationship load, understanding the Birth Order Effect will lighten that load and balance it. You'll discover that your partner wants to make the relationship work just as you do. That nagging fear you've lived with will be replaced by confidence in yourself and in your spouse.

It's going to turn the problems in your relationship into challenges. If you have felt that your partner doesn't understand you, birth order is going to bring about that understanding. You will be able to be yourself, feeling like you belong in your relationship instead of hanging on for fear of losing it. You can focus your hard work on positive goals and enjoy your spouse and your marriage.

The Birth Order Effect enables us to understand our own behavior and our partners'. Think of personality as a box—a container for our feelings, attitudes, behaviors, perceptions, coping strategies and expectations. Birth order allows us to understand what's in our box and why. Once we know those two things, we can identify the things we want to change, and then we can change them. And we can do it without feeling ashamed, guilty, inadequate, depressed or angry.

Just as important, birth order enables you to understand your partner. You'll be able to recognize your partner's sense of humor. You'll understand the source of your partner's jealousy. You'll correctly interpret your partner's way of expressing love for you. You'll know why your partner can't seem to relax and enjoy your relationship. No longer will you view your partner as purposely irritating, obstinate or obnoxious, because you'll be able to look into his or her birth order box and identify what's there and why. Communication and understanding will improve; irritation and conflict will decrease. Finally, you will be able to enjoy your partner, your marriage, and your life.

The Early Challenges

There are five birth order personalities: Only Child, First Born, Second Born, Third Born and Fourth Born. When we look at what each type of child has to deal with in the family, it's easy to see why these five birth order personalities develop the way they do and how they carry over into our adult lives.

The Only Child doesn't have any siblings to provide companionship or to distract Mom and Dad, so "Onlies" have to learn how to play alone without feeling lonely and how to cope with intrusion from parents. To deal with the first challenge, the Only Child develops a fertile imagination, inventing an imaginary friend or giving toys and pets human qualities to make up for the lack of companionship. Because the Only Child projects his or her own thoughts and feelings onto toys, pets and imaginary friends, the Only Child can organize and predict actions and reactions in his or her own world.

Unfortunately, Mom and Dad are not quite so predictable. Parents interrupt the Only Child's play. There are no brothers and sisters to share the spotlight, so the Only Child often feels smothered by his or her parents. As a result of parental intrusion, the Only Child will develop two speeds for doing things: Fun things get done fast so Mom and Dad don't have a chance to interfere, and boring things get done slowly so Mom and Dad will offer to help. And when things don't go according to plan, the Only Child will get frustrated.

ONLY CHILD CHARACTERISTICS INCLUDE:
- Waking up each day with a plan or schedule in mind
- Talking in terms of time and schedules ("It's time to …," etc.)
- Craving alone time
- Feeling frustrated when plans or schedules have to be changed, or when you're interrupted
- Making "to do" lists and crossing off, rather than checking off, items
- Feeling obligated to worry—about just about anything
- Expressing anger in quick explosions or tantrums

First Born children have a different set of challenges. There they were, the center of attention, and along comes this baby, stealing all of Mom and Dad's affection. From the First Born's point of view, it looks like Mom and Dad have transferred all their love to the second child, so First Borns have to cope with what they perceive to be a world without love. The only way they get Mom and Dad's attention any more is when they help with the baby or with household chores; then, the First Born will at least get a pat on the back and a "Good job!"

This experience teaches First Borns that the best they can hope for from others is approval, and First Borns will be careful to avoid any actions that might inspire disapproval. First Borns will say "I don't know" or "What do you think?" to avoid expressing a thought or preference that might offend someone else.

FIRST BORN CHARACTERISTICS INCLUDE:
◆ Worrying about offending others
◆ Feeling compelled to agree with others or have others agree with you
◆ Wanting to impress others
◆ Needing to know what other people think
◆ Being goal-oriented
◆ Daydreaming about future accomplishments, but putting off current tasks
◆ Feeling like you cannot get what you want

Second Born children have to learn how to cope with an older sibling who successfully competes for the parents' attention. The First Born is older and often outperforms the Second Born, leading the Second Born to feel woefully inadequate. To compensate for this, the Second Born child relentlessly pursues perfection; in the Second Born's world, there is no love unless one is perfect. The Second Born recognizes that it is impossible to be perfect in all areas, so he or she will typically choose one thing and will devote endless energy to becoming the best student, the best athlete, the best pianist or the best writer. Second Borns pay attention to details, search for flaws in just about everything, and tend to find fault with things and people. They welcome constructive criticism from others because this helps them in their progress toward perfection. Because this drive is so strong in Second Borns, they assume that everyone else is a perfectionist, too, and will offer unsolicited criticisms of their own. For Second Borns, nothing is ever really good enough.

SECOND BORN CHARACTERISTICS INCLUDE:
- Feeling that others don't care about your feelings
- Finding it hard to give or accept praise
- Suppressing your own feelings with logic
- Inability to accurately gauge others' feelings
- High sensitivity to anger and tension
- Evaluating others' words and actions
- Following rules

The Third Born has to learn how to deflect the Second Born's feelings of inadequacy, which the Second Born tries to pass onto the younger child. The Second Born may ridicule and disparage the Third Born, making the Third Born feel vulnerable. To cope with that feeling of vulnerability, the Third Born will develop a stoic façade to show the world that nothing bothers him or her. Third Borns whose older sibling is of the same sex will become fearless and will continually do things to prove they are not afraid. Third Borns whose older sibling is of the opposite sex will become fearful and will tend to avoid things that make them feel afraid or vulnerable.

THIRD BORN CHARACTERISTICS INCLUDE:
- Empathizing with the underdog
- Feeling pleased when others are pleased
- Keeping busy to avoid becoming bored
- Feeling offended when others don't listen to your ideas
- Making comparisons in your mind
- Spontaneity—changing plans at a moment's notice
- Having many acquaintances but only one or two close friends

The Third Born tries to pass on the feeling of vulnerability to the Fourth Born by telling the younger child that he or she is too small, too weak, too helpless, too ignorant or too incapable to play with the older kids. As a result, the Fourth Born struggles with a persistent feeling of immaturity and of being unwanted. If the Fourth Born can't overcome this feeling of immaturity, he or she will tend to withdraw from others. If the Fourth Born overcompensates by feeling super-mature, he or she may entertain others to be accepted.

FOURTH BORN CHARACTERISTICS INCLUDE:
- Feeling that life has to be hard
- Feeling left out
- Analyzing things from every angle
- Feeling suspicious when others are kind to you
- Feeling like you have to control your emotions
- Preferring to work hard
- Tendency to withdraw in large groups

Another interesting thing is that these birth order personalities are separate and distinct; they do not blend. Although we may exhibit traits of more than one Birth Order Personality, those traits are secondary and can appear and disappear almost at will. Our primary Birth Order Personality traits may vary in intensity, but they are consistent throughout our lives, regardless of what stage of life we are in.

What's Your Birth Order?

Now that you know a little bit about each of the birth order personalities, you may recognize common behaviors in friends or family members. But it might be harder for you to decide which Birth Order Personality is yours; most of us exhibit traits of more than one of the five birth orders, and sometimes it can be hard to judge which Birth Order Personality is our dominant one. As you become more familiar with each of the five personalities, recognizing each birth order's characteristics will become easier.

We have crafted three different quizzes to help you determine your Birth Order Personality. Two are relatively short and are designed to give a quick indication of your primary Birth Order Personality—the one that was formed in your first two to five years of life and that still provides your coping mechanisms when things get stressful.

But we have secondary birth order personalities, too. These are the behaviors we exhibit when life is running smoothly. So the third quiz is designed to measure both primary and secondary birth-order characteristics, giving you even deeper insight into your complete personality.

Remember that your psychological Birth Order Personality may or may not correspond to your chronological place in the family.

What Kind of Perfectionist Are You?

Alfred Adler, who first conceived the idea that birth order is related to personality development, thought that everyone—only children, oldest, middle and youngest—was always striving for perfection. The truth is, "perfection" means something different to each Birth Order Personality. This brief quiz will help you figure out what kind of perfectionist you are—and, therefore, which Birth Order Personality you have. Be as honest as you can and choose the one answer that fits you best.

1. In your "perfect world," which of the following would be true?
   a. Others would help you with tasks you find distasteful, but they would leave you alone to do the things you enjoy.
   b. Others would look up to you, respect your opinions and agree with your decisions.
   c. Everyone would follow the same rules, and others would offer suggestions on how to improve.
   d. Others would look to you for help, and they would be pleased with your efforts on their behalf.
   e. Others would invite you to join them in activities and would recognize how hard you work.

2. When you have to complete a project at work or at home, what do you like best about it?
   a. It's something you can do on your own.
   b. Others will be impressed with how well you do it.
   c. There are clear, step-by-step instructions to follow.
   d. Others will be pleased when you've finished.
   e. It won't be easy.

3. When you're working on a project at the office, which do you find most annoying?
   a. Your boss continually interrupts or makes suggestions on how to proceed.
   b. Your boss doesn't appear to be impressed.
   c. Your boss doesn't offer feedback.
   d. Your boss doesn't appear to be pleased with your work.
   e. Your boss doesn't understand the time and effort involved in the project.

4. When you've finished a major project, which gives you the greatest sense of accomplishment?
   a. You did it yourself.
   b. Others are impressed with your work.
   c. Others make suggestions to improve the final product.
   d. Others are happy with the result.
   e. You overcame difficulties through hard work.

5. When someone tells you something you've done is "perfect," which phrase best describes your reaction?
   a. I've done it right.
   b. I've earned the admiration of others.
   c. I think I could have done better.
   d. I've made others happy.
   e. I had to work hard, but it was worth it.

Scoring: If you answered "a" to three or more of the questions, your Birth Order Personality is that of the Only Child. You can be an Only even if you have one or more siblings, especially if there is a wide age gap between you and older or younger brothers and sisters. The Only Child is the one who has a fit when someone rearranges the things on her desk. She values order, resents intrusions and feels pressured when someone offers suggestions on how to do things. Almost all the time, the Only Child would rather work on his or her own; working with other people means a potential loss of order and increased pressure. To the Only Child, "perfection" is achieved when, in someone else's judgment, he or she has done something right.

If you answered "b" to three or more of the questions, you are a First Born personality. The First Born lost Mom and Dad's attention to the younger sibling and coped with that loss of attention by becoming a "little helper" to earn praise and affection from the parents. As adults, First Borns still equate admiration and respect with love, so they look for ways to impress other people with their skills and abilities. At work, the First Born will look for admiration and approval; at home, the First Born seeks respect. Disagreement to the First Born is a sign of disrespect; "perfection" means getting approval and praise and being looked up to.

If you answered "c" to three or more questions, you are a Second Born personality, the only one of the birth orders who seeks perfection for its own sake. Second Borns grow up dealing with the older First Borns, who always seem to be better at everything simply because they are older. Because Second Borns never can catch up to the First Borns, they seek out areas where they can be the best, and they devote all their energy to perfecting the area they've chosen. Sometimes they set impossibly high standards for themselves, so "good" is never good enough; unlike the Only, the Second Born welcomes suggestions for improvement as a way to move himself closer to perfection. In fact, a Second Born will be disappointed if he doesn't receive constructive criticism.

If you answered "d" to three or more questions, you are a Third Born personality. Your primary goal is to please others; you measure your success by whether you've made other people happy. To do this, the

Third Born has to be strong and capable of solving problems for others—skills the Third Born developed to deflect the teasing and criticism of the Second Born. Sometimes, the easiest way to make sure other people are happy is to let them do a project themselves. But if someone needs help, Third Borns are the first to volunteer, and they only achieve "perfection" when their efforts please other people.

If you answered "e" to three or more questions, you are a Fourth Born personality. When the older siblings did something fun and interesting, the Fourth Born was left behind because he or she was too little or too young to do anything. Even in adulthood, Fourth Borns still feel that others view them as immature, so they continually try to prove how grown-up they are by tackling difficult tasks. To the Fourth Born, an easy job isn't really worthwhile; "perfection" comes only from completing jobs that require lots of hard work.

How Do You Feel?

Each Birth Order Personality has its own way of dealing with emotions. This quiz measures how you feel most of the time. Answer the questions in each section with a yes or a no; for the most accurate reading, put down your first reaction.

Section I
1. Do you think with your feelings?
2. Do you feel pressured by interruptions?
3. Do you feel smothered by friends or family?
4. Do you feel compelled to organize time, people and things?
5. Is frustration your worst bad feeling?

Section II
1. Do you get confused when other people are talking?
2. Do you have trouble feeling grown-up?
3. Do you feel compelled to analyze others' words and actions?
4. Do you hesitate to join groups unless you're invited?
5. Do you feel you always have to work hard?

Section III
1. Do you have trouble knowing what you think, want or feel?
2. Do you often feel guilty, even if there's no reason to?
3. Do you feel relieved when you finish a task?
4. Do you feel compelled to find out what other people think?
5. Would you rather dream about the future than worry about today?

Section IV
1. Do you feel overly sensitive?
2. Do you like to pay attention to details?
3. Do you like being corrected when you are doing something?
4. Do your emotions overwhelm you as you try to control them?
5. Do you express anger by finding fault?

Section V
1. Do you have to be strong in order to feel safe?
2. Do you feel you must always compare things?
3. Do you feel you must help victims?
4. Do you feel you must always try to please other people?
5. Do you think it's strange that some people enjoy being afraid?

Scoring: The section that contains the most "yes" answers is your psychological birth order. Section I is Only Child; Section II is Fourth Born; Section III is First Born; Section IV is Second Born; and Section V is Third Born.

Birth Order Personality Inventory

This is the most detailed of the personality quizzes and will help you determine your primary and secondary birth order personalities. Because birth order is most evident during childhood and early adulthood, the accuracy of the test is enhanced if you answer the questions as you would have when you were in your late teens or early twenties.

Choose the answer that most nearly fits you for each question. When you've finished the questions, enter the number from each answer on the form at the end of the inventory and do the calculations to identify your birth order personalities.

1 = seldom   2 = sometimes   3 = often   4 = almost always

1. Do you have to put things in order before you can do something?
2. Do you have to make others think well of you?
3. Are you easily shamed?
4. Were your siblings unfair to you?
5. Do you like to work hard?
6. Do you make "to do" lists?
7. Do you say, "I don't know"?
8. Do you pay special attention to details?
9. Do you avoid scary things?
10. Are you suspicious of people?
11. Do you keep a time schedule in your head?
12. Are you afraid to offend others?
13. Do you hide your feelings?
14. Do you act like nothing bothers you?
15. Do you have to prove how mature you are?
16. Do you think with your feelings?
17. Do you picture how someone will react to you?
18. Do you look for flaws?
19. Do you have to be strong?
20. Does it feel like others don't want you?
21. Do you feel bad when others feel bad?
22. Do others' reactions make you feel guilty?
23. Do you say, "I would appreciate it if you would. . ."?
24. Do you relate well to victims?
25. Do you resent being asked for favors?
26. Do you interrupt when others are talking?

27. Do you picture how you should have acted?
28. Do you say, "That's not necessary"?
29. Do you jump to conclusions?
30. Do you feel like you're going to be trapped?
31. Do you worry about family and friends?
32. Do you think people should get what they deserve?
33. Do you like giving constructive criticism?
34. Do you like making comparisons?
35. Do you feel left out?
36. Do you like to have time at home alone?
37. Do you work hard to impress others?
38. Do you like to focus on one thing at a time?
39. Do you hate being teased?
40. Do you get angry at being blamed?
41. Does being interrupted frustrate you?
42. Are you too nice to people?
43. Do you dislike deadlines?
44. Do you say, "No problem!"?
45. Do you feel no one understands you?
46. How often do you feel frustrated?
47. Is it hard for you to express love?
48. Are you a sensitive person?
49. Are you looking for ways to help others?
50. Do you analyze things from all sides?
51. Are you afraid of appearing spoiled?
52. Is it difficult for you to feel loved?
53. Do you need to have well-defined projects?
54. Do you get angry when your idea is rejected?
55. Do you analyze questions before answering?
56. Do you feel smothered?
57. Are you afraid someone will be angry at you?
58. Do you hold back from giving compliments?
59. Do you keep busy to keep from being bored?
60. Do you feel like no one listens?

61. Do you do small projects before big projects?
62. Are you agreeable when you don't want to be?
63. Are you looking for perfection?
64. Do you hate being told to do something instead of being asked?
65. Do you try to control your anger?
66. Do you get upset when people drop in without advance notice?
67. Do you hint for what you want?
68. Does it anger you when someone accuses you of being nasty?
69. Is it important for you to please others?
70. Do you hate laziness in others?
71. Does life feel like all work and no play?
72. Do you compromise more than you should?
73. Are you a peacemaker?
74. Do you hate being cornered?
75. Do you get angry when others do nothing?

Scoring: Enter the number from each answer, and total each column:

A	B	C	D	E
1___	2___	3___	4___	5___
6___	7___	8___	9___	10___
11___	12___	13___	14___	15___
16___	17___	18___	19___	20___
21___	22___	23___	24___	25___
26___	27___	28___	29___	30___
31___	32___	33___	34___	35___
36___	37___	38___	39___	40___
41___	42___	43___	44___	45___
46___	47___	48___	49___	50___
51___	52___	53___	54___	55___
56___	57___	58___	59___	60___
61___	62___	63___	64___	65___
66___	67___	68___	69___	70___
71___	72___	73___	74___	75___

Total, Column A (Only Child)   _____

Total, Column B (First Born)   _____

Total, Column C (Second Born)   _____

Total, Column D (Third Born)   _____

Total, Column E (Fourth Born)   _____

Your highest score indicates your primary Birth Order Personality. The next two highest scores indicate secondary birth order characteristics.

Different birth order characteristics can clash or complement each other. When they clash, they can be the source of much unhappiness for couples who don't understand either their partner's behavior or the reasons behind it. In the next chapter, we look at how the birth order personalities typically interact and ways to enhance compatibility in your relationship.

CHAPTER TWO

The Birth Order Effect and Relationships

Webster's New World Collegiate Dictionary defines "compatible" as "capable of living together harmoniously or getting along well together." That's a good definition, but for our purposes here it doesn't go far enough. We define compatibility as the ability of two people to enjoy each other.

Enjoy is the key word in our definition. If we choose, all of us can get along with people we don't particularly like. But we enjoy our friends; we look forward to spending time with them and we consider that time well spent because we enjoy it.

If you think about the relationships in your life, this enjoyment component makes sense. A relationship is two people creating feelings in each other. If the feelings are good, the relationship will be good. If the feelings are bad, the relationship will be bad. And if there are no feelings, there is no relationship.

Compatibility = Equality

Think of your relationship as a seesaw, with your partner on one end and you on the other. The point of a seesaw is give and take: Sometimes you're up in the air, sometimes your partner is. As long as the seesaw keeps moving, each of you is getting the same amount of up and down time. But if the seesaw stops with one of you up in the air, there is no longer any give and take; equality is lost.

The ability to enjoy each other—to be compatible—requires an equal relationship. This means you relate to each other as individuals, with mutual respect and flexibility. If you and your partner aren't on an equal footing, neither of you is able to truly enjoy the other because too much of your energy is devoted to maintaining an awkward imbalance.

Inequality in a relationship can be caused by a number of factors—including the birth order coping strategies we developed as children:

◆ "Onlies" create unequal relationships when they project their own feelings onto their partners. This is the high end of the seesaw, when Onlies try to control others' emotions by "fixing" situations until others react the way the Only expects them to. On the low end of the seesaw, Onlies withdraw into their own worlds.

◆ First Borns put themselves on the high end of the seesaw when they demand unquestioning agreement from their spouses. Conversely, when First Borns insist on letting their spouses make all the decisions, they put themselves on the low end of the seesaw.

◆ Second Borns create unequal relationships when they try to "perfect" their partners. Even when a Second Born's criticism is constructive, it tends to set up a teacher-student dynamic, with the Second Born in the authoritative teacher's role—the high end of the seesaw. Second Borns are on the low end of the seesaw when they continually try to make peace with their partners.

◆ Third Borns create unequal relationships when they think of their partners as victims. This makes the entire relationship a rescue operation, with the Third Born responsible for solving problems—

the high end of the seesaw. Third Borns are on the low end of the seesaw when they work hard to please their partners.

♦ Fourth Borns create unequal relationships when they see their partners as possessions. This sets up the Fourth Born as "owner"; the one with decision-making power—again, the high end of the seesaw. The low end of the seesaw for Fourth Borns is passivity.

Notice how each Birth Order Personality has its own way of asserting control over others? Control can be subtle or overt. It can be dangerous or benevolent. Sometimes it's even necessary for one partner to take control. But it always, always skews the balance in a relationship, creating inequality.

Let's take the example of a Third Born woman who marries someone she feels sorry for. Her husband is the victim—not merely a victim of external forces, but also of his wife's pity. They cannot relate to each other as equals in these roles; he must rely on her to solve problems, and she must be strong in order to rescue him. There is no way for these two people to enjoy each other.

Whenever one partner feels like a victim, the other is automatically pushed into the role of either rescuer or persecutor. This is called the Drama Triangle, and it looks like this:

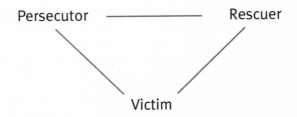

In this relationship, a person at the bottom of the triangle is powerless. He or she is at the mercy of the persecutor, the one who inflicts pain and anguish, or at the mercy of the rescuer, the one who solves all the problems. To the victim, it appears that the only way to escape the bottom of this triangle is to become a persecutor or a rescuer. But that automatically forces someone else into the victim's role, and this pattern of behavior becomes a never-ending cycle. The only way to restore balance—an equal relationship—is for both partners to abandon their roles in the Drama Triangle and relate to each other as individuals, and that can be very difficult, particularly if either (or both) of the partners is too accustomed to playing his or her respective role.

EXERCISE: Are you and your partner trapped in a Drama Triangle? Most relationships will spend brief periods in the Drama Triangle from time to time; when it becomes the day-to-day pattern, relationships are in trouble.

To find out if the Drama Triangle is dominating your relationship, consider the following questions. Be as honest as you can; answer "yes" only if the question describes typical behavior in your relationship. If these things don't happen on a regular basis, answer "no."

Part I—Are you a Rescuer, a Persecutor or a Victim?

1. When your partner takes on a new project or challenge, do you expect that he or she will need your help to succeed?
2. Do you become angry if your partner can't give you his or her undivided attention right away?
3. Do you routinely wait for your partner to make decisions affecting your relationship?

Part II – Is your partner a Rescuer, a Persecutor or a Victim?

1. When you make a suggestion for a new line of work, a change in décor or a project you want to try, does your partner say things like, "You can't do that," or "I can help you with that"?
2. Does your partner insist that you drop what you're doing when he or she needs your help or wants your attention?
3. Does your partner seem unable to make a decision without your assistance?

The first question in each section determines whether you are stuck in the Rescuer's role, or whether your partner is. The second question determines whether either of you are playing the Persecutor's role. The third question determines whether either of you are caught in the Victim's role. If you answered "yes" to any of these questions, you might be trapped in the Drama Triangle, and professional counseling may be in order.

Compatibility = Humor

Humor is an essential component of any relationship. It's a form of adult play, a way we enjoy each other and connect with each other. When couples lose their sense of humor with each other, the relationship is in trouble.

Humor also establishes equality in a relationship, because in order to appreciate each other's humor, both people must have comparable intelligence levels. That doesn't mean both have the same level of education. Schooling is not the same as intelligence, and intelligence doesn't have to be of the same kind to be comparable. One woman who was planning to go on to college was married to a man who could not read or write, but their intelligence levels were similar. At work, he could take a machine apart, reconfigure it, put it back together and have it working better than it did before. His genius was in his hands; hers was in academics.

Every relationship has some incompatibility. When differences arise, humor helps smooth out the bumps. Understanding birth order helps us understand each other's sense of humor and where it comes from. Without this knowledge, what is meant to be amusing can become irritating or hurtful.

Alan and Sarah learned this lesson the hard way. Alan is a Fourth Born and Sarah is an Only. This can be the most difficult of relationships because neither of these birth orders has an inherent understanding of the other. Both had been married before with the same Only/Fourth birth order combination, and these marriages had ended in divorce because they could not overcome their differences. But both Alan and

Sarah had come in for counseling during the break-ups of their first marriages and had learned about their own and their partner's birth order personalities. They brought this knowledge to their new relationship; in fact, it was what drew them together when one of them brought up the subject.

Armed with this insight into each other's personalities, Alan and Sarah are able to use humor to promote compatibility. Alan can joke about Sarah's organization, her tendency to worry, and other Only characteristics. Sarah can joke with Alan about his habit of analyzing everything, always trying hard, and other Fourth Born traits. Thus, they enjoy in each other what might otherwise be intolerable.

EXERCISE: Foibles are funny—if we look at them from the right angle. Problems arise when we are unable to get the proper perspective, and our own and our partner's foibles become major irritants. This exercise is designed to put some mental distance between you and the sources of irritation from your partner—to give you a different point of view. Watch a sitcom on TV or a funny movie and pay attention to the habits of the characters. Notice how those habits become the basis of humor in the show—how other characters react, what they say and do. Then think about the things your partner does that routinely irritate you—leaving dirty dishes in the sink, for example, or continually tinkering with the car, or putting the toilet paper on the roller the wrong way, or fidgeting. Try to match those things to sitcom or movie characters. If your partner fusses about clutter in the living room, for example, that would correspond to Monica on "Friends," who is a fanatical cleaner. If it helps, write down the irritating behavior and put the matching character's name next to that item. The next time your partner does that thing, think of the sitcom or movie character; with practice, you'll find your irritation giving way to amusement.

Do I Have an Ideal Mate?

Some of us spend years looking for Mr. or Ms. Right—as if finding a partner is like placing a piece in a jigsaw puzzle. The truth is, no relationship is 100 percent compatible 100 percent of the time. Sometimes we get angry, at each other or at the world; sometimes we succumb to stress, and our birth order coping strategies interfere with our compatibility; sometimes we lose our sense of humor and, with that, our ability to truly enjoy anything or anyone.

That said, there are factors that enhance compatibility. One very important factor is the relationship we have or had with our mothers (for women) and with our fathers (for men). Subconsciously, we tend to recreate that relationship with our partners. So, if a woman had a good relationship with her mother, she is likely to create a good relationship with her husband. If her relationship with her mother was rocky, chances are her marriage will be rocky, too.

For many of us, our "ideal partner" might be someone with the Birth Order Personality immediately following that of our same-sex parent. For instance, a Second Born woman with a Second Born mother might be most compatible with a Third Born man. Compatibility from this perspective is illustrated in the charts below for women and men.

"Ideal Partners" Chart

A compatible mate can be determined by matching your Birth Order Personality with your same-sex parent's Birth Order Personality. Except in the case of Onlies, the most compatible birth order is the one following your same-sex parent's Birth Order Personality.

Mother's Birth Order Personality

		Only	First	Second	Third	Fourth
Daughter's Birth Order Personality	Only	Only	First	Second	Third	Fourth
	First	Only	Second	Third	Fourth	Only
	Second	Only	Second	Third	Fourth	Only
	Third	Only	Second	Third	Fourth	Only
	Fourth	Only	Second	Third	Fourth	Only

Father's Birth Order Personality

Son's Birth Order Personality	Only	First	Second	Third	Fourth
Only	Only	First	Second	Third	Fourth
First	Only	Second	Third	Fourth	Only
Second	Only	Second	Third	Fourth	Only
Third	Only	Second	Third	Fourth	Only
Fourth	Only	Second	Third	Fourth	Only

Did you notice that First Borns don't appear in this chart very often? That's because First Borns have difficulty establishing a connection with other people; the exception is the First Born/Only relationship, particularly when the First Born is male.

Birth Order Interaction

Each birth order combination has its own set of strengths and weaknesses. Remember, our birth order personalities determine how we relate to each other, how we deal with emotions, how we communicate, and how we make decisions. Each Birth Order Personality is looking for its own source of satisfaction in a marriage:

- Onlies want to their partners to feel good so they can feel good (Onlies feel what those around them feel).
- First Borns want approval, admiration or respect (their substitutes for love), so they either tend to go along with their partners' wishes or try to impress their partners.
- Second Borns put the needs of their spouses and families before their own so they don't have to deal with negative feelings in their spouses and children.
- Third Borns want to please their spouses and children so they can feel safe.
- Fourth Borns want to give their families what they need so they can feel grown-up.

These certainly aren't bad attributes. But they can cause problems when we don't understand why our partners act the way they do. We explore the dynamics of each birth order combination in detail in later chapters. The following chart gives a quick sketch of what each birth order might like and dislike about the others.

ONLY/ONLY

The Only child lives in his or her own world. When two Onlies get married, often they live in separate worlds together. Each understands and has the same need for time alone, so they don't pressure each other. Both are organized and both dislike surprises, so their lifestyles usually are compatible. The area most likely to cause problems in an Only/Only relationship is communication: Each partner tends to project his or her own feelings and meaning onto the other, which can cause frustration.

ONLY/FIRST BORN

Onlies and First Borns can run into great difficulty in communication. The Only imagines what others think and feel, and First Borns are vague about what they think and feel. Nonverbal cues are critical to effective communication in this relationship. Interestingly, the Only/First Born relationship tends to be quite compatible when the woman is an Only and the man is a First Born. In this relationship, the First Born man appreciates the Only woman's ability to express herself, to be clear about what she wants, and to allow him to do what he wants. The Only woman doesn't feel pressured by the First Born man, and because he is unsure about what he thinks and feels, the Only woman can comfortably imagine what his thoughts and feelings are.

ONLY/SECOND BORN

Onlies and Second Borns are the most likely combination to experience "love at first sight." This also is the most common combination in marriage, and Only/Second marriages usually are quite successful. The Only expresses his or her emotions, but puts no pressure on the Second Born to share feelings. The Second Born's self-discipline and dependability allow the Only to be organized. However, the Second Born's perfectionist streak can frustrate the Only, and the Only's tendency to project—combined with the Second Born's aversion to emotions—can make both feel disconnected.

ONLY/THIRD BORN

Onlies and Third Borns often have a strong emotional connection. The Third Born finds it easy to please the Only and likes the emotional response from the Only; the Only finds the Third Born caring and empathetic. But the Third Born's spontaneity can cause great stress for the organized Only, and the Only's desire for time alone may lead to feelings of insecurity in the Third Born.

ONLY/FOURTH BORN

Onlies and Fourth Borns can have a wonderful relationship—if they realize from the beginning that neither has a gut-level understanding of the other. That's a big "if," though; both think they understand the other and both will get frustrated when the other doesn't behave as expected, so this combination can be the most difficult of all. The Only's imagination and the Fourth Born's creativity complement each other nicely. The Fourth Born's insulting type of humor meshes well with the Only's sarcasm. But while the Only is emotionally demonstrative, the Fourth Born tends to withdraw, and the Fourth Born's need to feel wanted might seem like an intrusion to the Only.

FIRST BORN/FIRST BORN

Two First Borns rarely get married; they don't have the emotional connection to attract them. When two First Borns do get together, the relationship can be an enduring one, though not necessarily a close one. Each would tend to seek good feelings from other people rather than from each other, and this lack of connection can lead to feelings of boredom and obligation.

FIRST BORN/SECOND BORN

This combination also seems to be rare, probably because the First Born finds the Second Born a little frightening. This can be a source of initial attraction, but with time the Second Born's criticisms, while meant to be helpful, feel like disapproval to the First Born, and the First Born's vagueness about what he or she wants can be irritating to the Second Born. As in the First Born/First Born relationship, emotional connection here is difficult because First Borns don't know how they feel and Second Borns try to quash their feelings.

FIRST BORN/THIRD BORN

This relationship poses a direct emotional challenge for the First Born. The First Born can find the Third Born's spontaneity and free emotional expression quite exhilarating, but may feel threatened by it over time. The Third Born is drawn to the First Born's dreams and goals, but may become unhappy with the lack of follow-through. It's easy for the Third Born to please the First Born because the First Born usually goes along with whatever the Third Born wants. The First Born's passiveness and the Third Born's aggression can cause problems in relating.

FIRST BORN/FOURTH BORN

This can be a difficult relationship for both, but it also can be very fulfilling if both understand birth order. The Fourth Born will tend to have the psychological upper hand in this relationship, and if the First Born tries to exert emotional power, it can set up a pattern of retaliation. If the Fourth Born understands that the First Born is out of touch with his or her feelings, the Fourth Born can provide direction for the relationship. But if the Fourth Born interprets the First Born's ambivalence as evasion, these two will have difficulty relating.

SECOND BORN/SECOND BORN

This tends to be a very compatible relationship, because the partners reinforce each other's perfectionist tendencies. Constructive criticism is welcomed by both, and logic, rather than emotion, is the guiding force. This relationship tends to minimize emotions, so overt conflict is rare. However, there might be a sense of competition between these two, which can exacerbate each partner's feelings of inadequacy.

SECOND BORN/THIRD BORN

If the Second Born doesn't require perfection from his or her partner, this combination can make for a very fulfilling relationship. The Second Born is drawn to the Third Born's freedom of emotional expression, but the Third Born's use of anger can upset and confuse the Second Born. The Third Born can get frustrated with the Second Born's attention to detail, which the Third Born finds boring. The Second Born's need to follow clearly defined rules and the Third Born's flair for breaking the rules can cause problems.

SECOND BORN/FOURTH BORN

These two birth orders can get along well because their thinking patterns—evaluation for the Second Born and analysis for the Fourth Born—complement each other. The Fourth Born's tendency to work hard appeals to the Second Born's self-discipline. If the Fourth Born carries a lot of anger, this relationship will be very stressful for the Second Born. The Second Born's emotional distance might feel like exclusion to the Fourth Born. The Second Born doesn't understand how the Fourth Born's mind works, which can be a source of conflict.

THIRD BORN/THIRD BORN

This may be the most compatible of relationships. These two work to please each other; they understand each other's thoughts and feelings. If one is a fearless-type Third Born and the other is a fearful type, they might fall into a rescuer-victim dynamic. Both will tend to be very nurturing and protective of their children. Because both are eager to help others and have difficulty setting boundaries, they may find themselves taken advantage of by others.

THIRD BORN/FOURTH BORN

The Third Born can find the Fourth Born a very stimulating partner, but the Fourth Born's ability to manipulate others can strike at the Third Born's sense of vulnerability. If the Fourth Born recognizes the Third Born's need to feel safe and is honest and trustworthy, this can be a very fulfilling relationship. The Third Born will work hard to please the Fourth Born, which helps the Fourth Born feel wanted. If the Fourth Born carries much anger, this will be a very difficult relationship.

FOURTH BORN/FOURTH BORN

Two Fourth Borns tend to work well together because they understand each other on a gut level. They appreciate each other's hard work and each other's sense of humor. Both will strive to give each other and their children what they need. When things get difficult, each will tend to withdraw from the other; this tendency can lead to serious communication problems and feelings of not being wanted.

INCREASING COMPATIBILITY

As we've said, no relationship is 100 percent compatible. But there are ways to encourage more compatibility. Perhaps most important is understanding birth order. When you know how each Birth Order Personality views the world, how each copes with stress, how each tries to relate to other people, and why each Birth Order Personality does these things, it takes a lot of the sting out of the differences that inevitably arise in close, long-term relationships. With these insights, you can stop viewing your partner as someone who intentionally tries to make life difficult and begin relating to each other as genuine human beings.

You'll find many of these insights right here, along with a wide range of tools designed to help you identify the strengths and weaknesses in your relationship and improve both the kind and quality of your connection with your partner.

Finally, never pass up a chance to learn. Talk to other men and women. Men, read women's magazines; women, read men's magazines. Find out what others have in their relationships and what they feel is missing. The more you know, the better prepared you are for those times when you and your partner seem less compatible than usual.

EXERCISE—HOW DO I ENJOY THEE? LET ME COUNT THE WAYS

Compatibility is the ability to enjoy each other. The following exercise is designed to measure how well you enjoy your partner's looks, feelings and behaviors. The first set of questions is for women; the second is for men. Rate each aspect of your partner on a scale of 1 to 10, with 10 representing the greatest enjoyment and 1 representing the least.

Women, how much do you enjoy:

1. The way he looks	1 2 3 4 5 6 7 8 9 10
2. The way he sounds when he talks	1 2 3 4 5 6 7 8 9 10
3. The way he responds to you	1 2 3 4 5 6 7 8 9 10
4. The way he treats you in public	1 2 3 4 5 6 7 8 9 10
5. The way he treats you in private	1 2 3 4 5 6 7 8 9 10
6. The way he interacts with others	1 2 3 4 5 6 7 8 9 10
7. The way he feels about himself	1 2 3 4 5 6 7 8 9 10
8. His mannerisms	1 2 3 4 5 6 7 8 9 10
9. The way he dresses	1 2 3 4 5 6 7 8 9 10
10. The way he makes you feel	1 2 3 4 5 6 7 8 9 10
11. The way he thinks	1 2 3 4 5 6 7 8 9 10
12. The way he relates to other women	1 2 3 4 5 6 7 8 9 10
13. The way he understands you	1 2 3 4 5 6 7 8 9 10
14. Trusting him	1 2 3 4 5 6 7 8 9 10
15. Being with him	1 2 3 4 5 6 7 8 9 10

Men, how much do you enjoy:

1. The way she looks	1 2 3 4 5 6 7 8 9 10
2. The way she sounds when she talks	1 2 3 4 5 6 7 8 9 10
3. The way she responds to you	1 2 3 4 5 6 7 8 9 10
4. The way she treats you in public	1 2 3 4 5 6 7 8 9 10
5. The way she treats you in private	1 2 3 4 5 6 7 8 9 10
6. The way she interacts with others	1 2 3 4 5 6 7 8 9 10
7. The way she feels about herself	1 2 3 4 5 6 7 8 9 10
8. Her mannerisms	1 2 3 4 5 6 7 8 9 10
9. The way she dresses	1 2 3 4 5 6 7 8 9 10
10. The way she makes you feel	1 2 3 4 5 6 7 8 9 10
11. The way she thinks	1 2 3 4 5 6 7 8 9 10
12. The way she relates to other men	1 2 3 4 5 6 7 8 9 10
13. The way she understands you	1 2 3 4 5 6 7 8 9 10
14. Trusting her	1 2 3 4 5 6 7 8 9 10
15. Being with her	1 2 3 4 5 6 7 8 9 10

On each set of questions, total the numbers from your answers.

120 points or higher: You may be almost perfectly compatible, or you might not be seeing each other clearly.

90–119 points: Your relationship is pretty compatible. There may be some areas you can work on to increase your ability to enjoy each other.

89 or lower: Are you being too critical of your partner, or does your relationship need some help? Try to remember when you enjoyed your partner more, and ask yourself what, if anything, has changed since then. You might benefit from professional counseling.

If both you and your partner do this exercise and one score is high and the other is low, it may mean that the one with the lower score is in the relationship for the sake of the other person—not really enjoying the other person, but sacrificing his or her own happiness for the other's sake. Different birth order personalities will do this for different reasons. The Only will stay because he or she cannot stand to see the other person unhappy. The First Born will stay because he or she cannot offend the other person by leaving. The Second Born will stay because the commitment he or she feels is a rule that can't be broken. The Third Born will stay to please the other person. The Fourth Born will stay to make it easy for the other person.

Now it's time to take an in-depth look at each of the birth order personalities and how they relate to each other. We start in the next chapter with the Only Child.

CHAPTER THREE

The Only Child

T he Only Child never lacks for companionship. From a very early age, the Only Child had to learn how to play alone without feeling lonely; to accomplish this, Onlies develop fertile imaginations and vivid fantasy lives, densely populated with interesting playmates. These playmates might be human or animal, animate or inanimate. Often, an Only Child's possessions will take on lives of their own, complete with names, distinct personalities and (because the Only Child imagines them) completely predictable reactions.

That predictability is important to the Only Child. It helps him stay organized and, frankly, predictable imaginary behavior is a lot easier to deal with than unpredictable real-life behavior. In many cases, Onlies prefer being with their things over being with other people; people aren't nearly so well organized as the Only's possessions.

A good, though unintentional, example of the Only's preference can be found in the 1979 Steve Martin comedy, *The Jerk*. Martin's character has had a bad day: He lost a lawsuit, his business is bankrupt, and, on top of all that, he's having a huge fight with his wife. He threatens to leave, telling his wife, "I don't need you. I don't need anything except this," as he picks up an ashtray. "The ashtray, the paddle game, and the remote control, and that's all I need."

The truth is, at times, possessions really are the only things an Only Child needs. An adult Only Child left alone in the house rarely feels lonely because the possessions are there, comfortable and comforting. Possessions never argue with you; they stay where you put them; they don't pressure you to do things you don't want to do; they are true and staunch friends.

This attachment to things can appear a little odd from outside the Only Child's perspective. Onlies are likely to name their vehicles—one Only called his first new car "the little brown horse" —and may even refer to giving their vehicles "a bath" instead of washing them. Onlies imbue their things with human emotions and imagine that their possessions feel lonely or neglected if they don't spend enough time with them. After a trip, an Only may come into the house, pick up a favorite item and coo, "I missed you!" If an item is out of place, be prepared for an outburst of frustration: Onlies don't like it when other people mess with their things because it upsets their sense of organization.

The Only's lively imagination extends to other people. It's so easy for the Only Child to project his or her feelings, thoughts and motives onto possessions that doing it to other people just comes naturally. In a sense, people in an Only's life are imaginary, too—the Only imagines how those people feel, what they think, how they'll act or react, and the reasons behind what they do. When people don't feel, think, act or react the way the Only expects them to, the Only may become frustrated or may try to "fix" the situation until his or her expectations are met.

Getting the Only in your life to relate to you in the real world can be challenging, but if you understand what's going on in the Only's unique world, it can be intensely rewarding.

EXERCISE: Imagine you are two years old, sitting in the middle of the floor and surrounded by toys. You carefully place each toy where you want it. There may not be much order to your placement from an adult point of view, but they are organized the way you decide to organize them. Now imagine an adult comes along and decides to help you place some adult-style order on your toys. You protest; you may even snatch a toy away from the adult and put it back where you had it in the first place. Feel how frustrating it is to have someone else interfere with something you were doing, and how helpless you feel when the adult continues to interfere. When you can clearly picture this scene and the feelings that arise from it, you are experiencing what it feels like to be an Only Child.

This Goes Here, That Goes There

Just as nature abhors a vacuum, Onlies abhor disorganization. Whether it's tools in the garage, files at work, or spices in the kitchen cupboard, the Only needs to know that everything is where it belongs. This doesn't necessarily mean the Only is a neatnik. Files on the Only's desk may be piled in an apparently haphazard fashion, but we guarantee you the Only will know which files belong in that pile and which don't.

Organization gives Onlies both control over and comfort in their own worlds, and they will attempt to organize anything and everything. Once they get something organized, whether it's their schedule for the day, the tackle box for fishing, or the seating chart for a fancy dinner party, that organization is set in stone for the Only. Should anything come along to disrupt the Only's plan—a late start in the morning, a shortage of fishing line or an extra guest for the party—the Only is likely to feel that the whole thing is spoiled and must be started over. The outburst of frustration from an Only under these circumstances can appear to be completely out of proportion to other birth orders, but it is a very serious matter to the Only.

One Only man on a camping trip with his family felt that the entire trip had been spoiled when a strong rain storm blew their tent down and snapped a couple of the tent poles. They were halfway through a three-week trip, some 1,100 miles from home, and this Only man felt like the entire vacation had been ruined by the mishap. "That's it, we have to go home," he announced to his family. Fortunately, the man's son was a former Boy Scout; he found some saplings and used them to connect the tent poles until more permanent repairs could be made. The Only father was able to get reorganized around this temporary fix, and the family continued their vacation.

EXERCISE: Believe it or not, Onlies can learn to enjoy disorganization—if they can plan for it. Build some planned chaos into your schedule as a reward for all the organizing you do the rest of the time—say half an hour a day to start. This planned chaos is completely free time—no schedule and no imagining what you're going to do during this time. You can do whatever you feel like doing at the moment. At first, this unscheduled time might feel awkward and uncomfortable, but it will get a little easier each day. You might even come to enjoy it enough that you want to build more planned chaos into your schedule!

If You Feel Bad, I Feel Bad

Onlies' feelings are often tied up in what others around them are feeling. This symbiotic emotional connection can lead Onlies into the role of "fixer" when others feel bad: Onlies want the people around them to feel good so they can feel good themselves.

The son of the Only father who wanted to go home when the tent poles broke also is an Only Child personality, even though he has a younger sister. His father's anger made his mother and sister unhappy, which in turn made the son unhappy. He would be able to feel better only if the rest of the family felt better, so he had to find a way to "fix" the situation so that everyone could be happy again. His creative solution to the problem accomplished just that: Dad calmed down, which allowed Mom and Sis to relax, and the son felt better because everyone else felt better.

Onlies also don't like to be the reason for someone else feeling bad. Every Christmas, one Second Born girl dreaded helping her father, an Only, put up the Christmas tree. The girl knew that getting the tree to stand straight would be a struggle, and she knew that if they had a lot of trouble with the tree, her father would get angry and would shout and swear. Second Borns are particularly sensitive to anger. Even though the Only's anger usually is a quick outburst to express frustration and is over as suddenly as it comes, the Second Born girl always felt nervous when she knew her father was likely to get angry.

One year, the girl asked her father if he would try to put up the Christmas tree without swearing. The father was surprised that his daughter remembered his frustration from past Christmases, because to him those incidents of anger were long over and done with. However, now that he knew that his expressions of anger made his daughter feel bad, he made a special effort to contain his frustration.

As commendable as it might be to want everyone around you to feel good, others don't always appreciate the Only's efforts to "fix" things. Sometimes, people need to express their feelings just so others will understand what's going on with them. This can be a blind spot for the Only, and if the Only persists in trying to "fix" his or her partner's feelings, the partner will likely feel that the Only isn't really listening or taking the partner's feelings seriously.

EXERCISE: Onlies tend to hear a request for action in nearly everything other people say to them. If the other person is discussing a problem with his or her car, the Only will offer advice on how to fix it or recommend a good mechanic—regardless of whether the other person already knows how to fix it or already has a trusted mechanic. To counter this tendency if you are an Only, ask yourself three questions: Can I fix this? Should I fix this? Does the other person want me to fix this? If the answer to any of these questions is "no," then the other person just wants to talk, and you can step out of "fixing" mode. If you aren't sure whether someone is asking you to fix something, simply ask, "Do you want my (help/advice)?"

If your partner is an Only who tends to try to fix things when you just want to talk, preface your comments with, "I just want to talk about this." This phrase tells the Only how to please you, which takes pressure off the Only.

What I Mean Is . . .

In the Only Child's imaginary world, making your meaning clear isn't necessary because you and others can always intuit the meaning behind any set of words or behavior. You know what others are thinking and others know what you're thinking, so you don't have to spell things out. You don't even have to finish your sentences if you don't want to, in the Only Child's world.

In the real world, this Only Child trait can get in the way of genuine communication. Onlies will often interrupt others because they think they already know what the other person is going to say. And Onlies often won't say exactly what they mean, but something close to it, assuming that others will be able to understand them. An Only rarely will say, "Let's turn the furnace up." Instead, he or she is more likely to say something like, "It's cold in here, isn't it?" or "Aren't you cold?" Notice that both of these questions anticipate a "yes" answer. If the other person says no, the Only will be genuinely surprised; the Only already has guessed how the other person feels, and if that guess is wrong, it completely disorganizes the Only.

Likewise, Onlies attach their own meaning to what others say. If an Only's spouse says, "It's cold in here," the Only very likely will turn the thermostat up even as the spouse is putting on a sweater. To the Only, even a simple statement like this is really a request to take action, to "fix" or organize the situation.

Onlies also interpret concepts common to other birth order personalities to fit their own perceptions. For example, First Borns tend to feel guilty when they think they've offended someone. Onlies adjust this concept of guilt so that it means the same thing as the Only feeling of guilt over not getting things done. Second Borns feel inadequate because they believe others can do things better than they can, but Onlies translate inadequacy as not being able to do what they want. The Third Born sense of vulnerability is transformed into the Only's tendency to worry about what might happen. And the Fourth Born concept of feeling trapped mutates into the Only's feeling of being required to do something. Thus, even when they use the same words, Onlies and other birth order personalities mean different things, and this fundamental lack of communication can be very frustrating for both.

EXERCISE: Onlies tend to live in their own world, so they are often oblivious to how the people around them feel. They also tend to assume that others know what they are thinking and feeling. This exercise will help break this tendency.

Today, when you and your partner are together, pay close attention to each other. Note the non-verbal communication—facial expressions, eye movement, gestures, and so on. When you think you know what your partner is thinking or feeling, test yourself with these phrases:

- "You look like you are (happy, sad, tired, relaxed, or whatever you think you observe)."
- "You sound like you (could use a break, need a hand, or whatever meaning you think you hear behind your partner's words)."
- "You act like you are (interested, frustrated, excited, or whatever attitude you think you perceive)."

Keep your comments on a positive note, and remember that you might be wrong in your interpretation. Listen to your partner's correction. Pay attention also to your partner's reaction to your feedback. You may find that he or she is pleased with your observation, even if your interpretation is wrong. Your partner may be especially pleased with being able to give you honest feedback about himself or herself—not based on what each of you imagine or assume.

All Work and No Play

When they were children, Onlies developed two speeds for doing things. Things they enjoyed were done quickly, so that parents or others wouldn't have a chance to intrude. Things they didn't enjoy were done slowly in hopes that parents or others would offer to help.

As adults, Onlies still have these two speeds for doing things, although they may train themselves to do distasteful things hastily to get them over with. In general, though, Only adults tend to have fun quickly and do work slowly, and, as a result, it feels to the Only like there is less time for fun. This problem is exacerbated by the Only's difficulty in separating work from play. When Onlies are working, they often think about all the fun things they'd rather be doing. When they're having fun, they tend to worry about the work that needs to be done. At play, Onlies don't really relax enough to genuinely enjoy themselves; work is always hanging around in the background, making the Only feel guilty for leaving it undone.

When the Only does want help with a project, he or she may not come right out and ask for it. Instead, there might be only a hint, a sort of invitation to another person to offer assistance. If an Only says, "Boy, this kitchen is a mess," or, "This closet needs to be cleaned out," he or she may be waiting for you to offer your help. If you don't offer to help, or if you can't help right now, be prepared for an outburst of frustration. When Onlies make this kind of invitation, it means two things: First, they've gone through an internal struggle and are admitting, in their own way, that they cannot or don't want to do it themselves, and, second, they've organized themselves around the idea of having help at the time they plan to complete their work. The internal struggle itself can generate anger in the Only, and the disruption of the schedule only adds to the anger.

One Only woman had such an outburst when she asked her husband to help her move a heavy box. He was on the Internet and wanted to finish what he was doing, so he said, "I can't right now. I'll help you later." The woman got disgusted, said, in classic Only language, "Forget it, I'll do it myself," and then struggled to get the box moved to where she wanted it. She was organized to do the job right then, and she couldn't tolerate changing her schedule—especially since her husband didn't tell her when he could help her so she could reorganize her time.

Fortunately, these outbursts are usually short-lived, and Onlies generally do not retain their anger. In fact, such incidents often become the basis for Only humor in the future. The next time this woman's husband talks about helping her with a chore, she is likely to respond with, "Sure, like you helped me with that box."

EXERCISE: Onlies tend to view time as a limitation rather than a resource; they feel they don't have enough time to do the things they want to do. You can make time into a resource by building extra time into your schedule. If you think it will take you thirty minutes to clean the kitchen, for example, allow forty-five minutes. If you expect to spend two hours at a nice restaurant for dinner before you go to the movie, give yourself an extra thirty minutes. By padding your schedule like this whenever you can, you'll feel less rushed, and you'll be more relaxed because you'll have time to finish what you're doing.

The Only and Other Onlies

Two Onlies live in separate worlds together. They tend to be very comfortable with each other, because they understand each other. They don't argue as such; they may blow up at each other once in a while, but the storm passes quickly and usually doesn't leave any mess behind. Onlies don't try to corner each other; they don't issue ultimatums; they don't try to force the other to do things. Each understands the other's need for time alone and for an organized schedule, and neither feels threatened by these needs. And each understands what the other means, even when that meaning isn't spelled out.

This is the one birth order combination that doesn't seem to require bonding for a happy relationship, although bonding always helps. One couple, both Onlies, met and married within three days. Their careers took them away from each other for extended periods, but this didn't cause problems for them. Their relationship endured, in part because each projected his or her own thoughts and feelings on the other. And, because they were both Onlies, those projections were pretty close to the mark.

Onlies can bond, but they tend not to do the things that encourage bonding. Onlies don't like to make plans too far in advance because they don't know whether they'll feel like doing an activity when the time comes. And an unplanned activity can interfere with the Only's mental schedule, causing frustration. This is what happened to Adam and Joy, two Onlies who never seemed to be able to date after they moved in together. Adam would suggest going out to dinner, and Joy would say, "I don't feel like it tonight. You can go out with Jim if you want." Joy would suggest going to visit her parents, and Adam would say, "I have some things I want to do around here. You go and say hi to them for me." This worked for them because each enjoyed the time alone, but it meant that they seldom went out together and so missed lots of opportunities to strengthen their bond.

The lack of bonding can become apparent when a relationship between two Onlies comes to an end. One Only woman who had been married for several years to another Only had difficulty getting her husband to help her with the care and raising of their children. This couple did a lot of talking, but very little real communicating. Their comments in a conversation were reflections of their own perceptions, rather than the result of truly listening to what the other person was saying. They talked at each other instead of with each other, and they couldn't solve problems together. Eventually the woman decided she had had enough and she filed for divorce. She was very matter-of-fact about the end of her marriage—unusual for an Only who thinks with her feelings. The lack of bonding in her marriage made it easy for her to leave; there was no emotional connection and so the break-up could not cause her pain.

For Angela and Clint, the lack of bonding maintenance contributed to their break-up. For the ten years of their marriage they had seemed to get along well, but Clint had allowed his addictive personality to take over his life. He was addicted to alcohol, to sixteen-hour workdays, and to sports, which he watched whenever he had a free moment. There was no time left for family. The marriage endured for so long because Angela was an Only and could tolerate being alone.

But when another man began paying attention to her, Angela realized what she had been missing. This other man created good feelings in her, while Clint created none at all, good or bad. Angela decided to divorce Clint.

When she told him, Clint panicked. It turned out he was as addicted to Angela as he was to other things in his life. He went in for counseling and tried to use what he learned there to pressure Angela into staying. But his concern even then was not for her needs but for his own. He felt bad about her leaving; therefore she should stay so he could feel better. The pressure Clint put on Angela only made her want to get out of the relationship faster.

EXERCISE: Onlies don't like to plan too far in advance, but without a schedule, Onlies tend to neglect doing the things that strengthen and nurture their bond with each other. To address this, make a weekly schedule for you and your partner that includes at least one activity for you to do together away from the house and at least one block of two or more hours for each partner to have the house to himself or herself. Limit this schedule to a week at a time; if you try to do it for longer periods, you are less likely to follow it because you won't feel like it by the third or fourth week. A weekly schedule allows the Only to organize his or her thinking. Scheduling time together away from the house and time at home alone addresses both the need for bonding between Onlies and each partner's need for private time.

The Only and the First Born

Onlies and First Borns tend to get together when they're young. After their teens or very early twenties, these two birth orders generally won't find enough to attract them to each other, in part because with age we tend to think more critically and expect more from our partners.

When Onlies and First Borns do get together, the result can be an enduring, if sometimes rocky, relationship. This combination tends to be easier when the woman is the Only Child; Only men are more goal-oriented and need feedback from their partners, but First Born women don't know what they think or feel and so are unable to supply that feedback. By contrast, Only women are able to organize themselves around First Born men and don't require the same kind of feedback that their male counterparts need.

The area with great potential for conflict, or at least misunderstanding, is the concept of pleasing your partner. Onlies want their partners to be happy because then they can feel happy, and they will work hard to accomplish this. However, since First Borns don't know what they want, the Only often has to guess, and this can lead to problems.

That's what happened to Steve and Julie. They met when they were in their early teens and became constant companions, doing all the things that teenagers do together and developing a powerful bond. But, often, Steve had to guess at what Julie wanted because she was unable to tell him. Their conversations would go something like this:

"Julie, would you like to see a movie tonight?" Steve would ask.

"I don't care. I guess that would be OK," she would reply.

"What movie do you want to see?"

"I don't know. Whatever you want to see is OK with me."

"How about the movie showing at the Rialto?"

"Yeah, we can go see that."

Steve was at sea because he couldn't find out exactly what Julie wanted. He wanted her to be happy, but he had no way of knowing what to do. On the rare occasions when she did express an opinion, Steve was delighted that he finally had something to work with. But because these occasions were so few and far between, Steve had difficulty distinguishing between Julie's fantasies and what she really wanted. When she told him that she had thought about running away, Steve thought this was a genuine desire of hers, so he made it happen. They ran away together; Julie went along because she didn't know what she really wanted to do. A few days later, they were found in a distant state and returned to their homes, but Steve didn't give up. He believed Julie really wanted to run away, so he arranged another escape. This time the law separated them and they didn't see each other for several years.

When they met again, Julie had been through two brief marriages and Steve had done a stint in the Army. The old bonding between them took hold again; they fell in love and got married.

But the pattern hadn't changed. Steve still wanted to make Julie happy, but he didn't know what she wanted because she didn't know herself. Steve pounced on every tiny clue, taking the most casual statements as proof of Julie's desires and acting on them in hopes that it would make her happy.

One day, Julie expressed admiration for a very macho male. Steve, thinking that this was what she really wanted, became macho himself. He let his hair grow long, rode motorcycles, began talking in short, curt phrases and took to acting like nothing bothered him. But, because he was no longer himself, Steve and Julie couldn't connect. With nothing to sustain it, their powerful bond decayed, and, after the children were grown, Steve and Julie went their separate ways. After the divorce, Steve dropped the macho façade. He didn't need it to please Julie any more; he could be himself again.

EXERCISE: Onlies and First Borns who want to please each other can have a terrible time communicating—with the result that neither is very happy. If you're an Only, you can encourage your First Born partner to tell you what he or she wants by saying, "I want you to (choose a movie or a restaurant, etc . . .)" This phrase tells the First Born how to please you.

If you're a First Born, you can encourage your Only partner to stop guessing at what you want by asking him or her to make the decision: "Would you pick out a movie for us to see?" With this phrase, the Only knows how to "fix" the problem and doesn't have to guess.

The Only and the Second Born

Onlies and Second Borns are the most likely birth orders to experience love at first sight. The Only's emotional expression and attention to detail in telling stories appeals to the Second Born, while the Second Born's dependability and willingness to give his or her partner "alone" time seem heaven-sent to the organized Only. But these two personalities can grate on each other, too. The Second Born's continual correction puts pressure on the Only, and the Only's tendency to guess at what the Second Born wants can make the Second Born feel misunderstood.

Ginny and Rob nearly divorced because of Rob's "constructive criticism." As an Only, Ginny resented correction; it made her feel like she couldn't do things right, and that in turn made her feel pressured to do things right. Rob, like most Second Borns, assumed others shared his drive for perfection and offered his criticisms in what he thought was a helpful manner, intended to assist Ginny in moving toward perfection. Every night, when he came home from work, he always had a critical comment to make, never a compliment. He would remark that the bookshelves needed to be dusted, but he wouldn't comment on the sparkling clean bathroom. He would suggest ways for Ginny to manage her time better, but he wouldn't commend her for juggling a career, the kids and the running of the household. Eventually, this continual criticism disheartened Ginny so much that she finally announced she wanted out of the marriage.

The effect of her announcement was almost magical. Rob suddenly became aware of Ginny's feelings—something Second Borns aren't naturally good at—and began to look for ways to make her feel good about him and about their relationship. It was awkward at first, because giving compliments doesn't come naturally for Second Borns either, but Rob began to pay attention to Ginny's feelings and he got better with practice. In the end, he learned to enjoy giving Ginny positive feedback. Ginny didn't feel pressured any more, and both of them learned to enjoy each other again.

Because they are so used to imagining how others feel, Onlies also have a blind spot when it comes to paying attention to others' feelings. Alan, an Only, and Jennifer, a Second Born, fell in love at first sight. They were so compatible that neither had to work very hard to understand the other. Enjoying each other came naturally, and they reveled in it. When they were ready to be married, Alan was so excited and happy to have Jennifer as his wife that he planned a special surprise for her: He remodeled his house so that it would be beautiful for her when she moved in. He expected her to be happy with the home he provided for her. When she became depressed and unmotivated, Alan felt confused and unhappy. He didn't understand that Jennifer would have been happier if remodeling the house had been her project, or something they did together. Because Alan assumed that Jennifer would want what he wanted, Jennifer felt that Alan didn't really understand her and didn't want her input. Things improved when they began having children. Jennifer recovered from her depression because she and Alan raised the children together.

EXERCISE: The Second Born's continual quest for perfection feels like pressure to the Only, who just wants to do things right the first time. If you're an Only, you can counter your Second Born's correction by saying, "This may not be perfect, but . . ." This lets the Second Born know that "good enough" is OK for now.

If you're a Second Born and you want your Only partner to pay attention to what you really mean, say, "I don't know about you, but..." This alerts the Only that you might have a different opinion or idea.

The Only and the Third Born

Onlies and Third Borns are attracted to each other because both have strong emotional components in their personalities. The difference between these two birth orders is that Onlies think with their feelings, and Third Borns act from their feelings. And this can cause conflict.

When Onlies think with their feelings, they are really organizing their behavior, even their schedule, around how they feel. They make plans based on how they feel and how others around them feel. But for Third Borns—especially fearless Third Borns—how they feel can change at a moment's notice, and consequently their behavior changes just as quickly, regardless of plans or schedules. The Third Born's spontaneity can be intolerable to the organized Only; likewise, the Only's organization can feel restrictive to the Third Born, who will become bored.

If an Only refuses to be drawn out of his or her own world, a relationship with a Third Born can be doubly frustrating for both partners. That's what has happened with Rick, an Only, and Kim, a fearless Third Born, both in their early 40s. Throughout the ten years of their marriage, Rick has been in his own world, a closed system impervious to Kim's efforts to make him understand how she feels and what she wants. Because she is a fearless Third Born, Kim attacks Rick to make her point, which just puts Rick on the defensive. Finally, in a desperate effort to get through to him, Kim moved out. She doesn't want to end the marriage. She wants to repair it. But she could think of no other way to make Rick take their problems seriously.

Rick agreed to counseling, but for some time he continued to live in his own world, imagining how Kim was feeling and what she was thinking without ever really listening to what she tried to tell him. On his own, and without any indication from Kim that this was what she wanted or intended, Rick decided that Kim would move back home after Christmas. When she didn't, he became depressed and passed his bad feelings onto her and their children. He apologized for his behavior, but he justified it on the basis of his feelings. In other words, he couldn't help how he felt when she didn't conform to his plan of moving back home.

Clearly, Kim and Rick still had problems communicating. In counseling, whenever Kim had some criticism, Rick would throw his hands up in a defensive gesture and interrupt her, saying, "I know, I know." Kim felt Rick wasn't listening to her, and she was right.

On her part, Kim often took offense at things Rick said because she would put her own interpretation on his words. As an Only, Rick doesn't say exactly what he means, just something close to what he means. When Kim assigned her own interpretation to his words, Rick was again on the defensive, having to explain that her interpretation was not what he meant.

To open up the lines of communication, Rick had to learn to really listen to what Kim was saying instead of assuming that he already knew what she was going to say. Kim had to learn to ask Rick what he meant by what he said instead of assigning her own meaning to his words. Understanding birth order and how it affects their behavior is helping Rick and Kim learn to communicate better and to understand each other's view of the world.

Greg and Beth are also in counseling to better understand each other and their own birth order personalities. Greg, an Only, had been attracted to a Second Born woman, but his parents didn't approve of her. They did approve of Beth, a fearless Third Born. As an Only who wanted to do what was right and who didn't want to upset his parents, Greg decided to marry her. He had misgivings, even at the wedding, but he talked himself out of those bad feelings, telling himself that Beth was a good person and that his parents were right.

From the outside, the marriage was good. Greg and Beth both came from stable homes, so they created harmony in their own home. They took care of their finances, didn't abuse alcohol or drugs, built good careers and had two beautiful children. Everything was perfect—except that Greg was discontent.

Things came to a head when Greg and Beth passed their twenty-sixth birthdays. This is one of the life passage points that all of us go through. It is when we stop believing in magic and fairy tales and begin to take responsibility for our own lives. After Greg's twenty-sixth birthday, he finally admitted that he was unhappy with his life, good as it was. He knew that if he left his marriage, others wouldn't understand; on the surface, his relationship with Beth seemed perfect, and everyone would think he was crazy if he threw it away.

He decided not to leave Beth. Instead, he decided to try to improve his relationship with her. They began dating again to improve their bond. Greg admitted that when he went home, he felt as if a weight had settled on his shoulders, and when he left the house, the weight lifted—a typical Only feeling. To bond, he and Beth had to get away from the house.

They also agreed to long-term counseling to help them better understand each other. At first, Beth didn't see the need for it because, from her perspective, everything was fine. But once she understood how Greg felt, she agreed to it. As they learn more about birth order, Greg and Beth are beginning to realize how little they truly understand each other and the dynamics of their personalities. It is uphill work for each, and only time will tell whether counseling and understanding birth order will be enough to make the relationship emotionally satisfying for both of them.

EXERCISE: When we say "I know" in response to what someone else has said, what we really mean is, "Don't tell me any more because I already know." And that means we aren't willing to listen. When Onlies say, "I know," it means they already have attached their own meaning to what others are saying. To get your Only partner to listen to you, say, "Pay attention to what I'm saying." This takes the Only out of his or her own world and brings focus to what you are trying to communicate.

If you don't understand what your Only partner is trying to say, ask, "What do you mean?" This lets the Only know that you need more information and he or she will respond with it.

If you're an Only and your Third Born partner misinterprets your words, say, "That's not what I mean. Please listen." Then put your feelings in different words to help the Third Born correctly interpret your message.

The Only and the Fourth Born

This can be one of the most difficult birth order combinations and is the one most likely to lead to emotional and physical abuse, especially if the Fourth Born in the relationship carries much anger.

Part of what makes this relationship so difficult is that the thinking patterns of Onlies and Fourth Borns are diametrically opposed to each other. Onlies like to organize things. They like to tie up all the loose ends and wrap everything up in a neat package so they can mentally put it away and not have to think (or worry, to use the Only's favorite word) about it anymore. Fourth Borns, on the other hand, are analytical thinkers. They ask lots of "what if" questions, and they put off reaching conclusions until their analysis is complete. This, of course, can take some time, and as a result there are usually quite a few loose ends in the Fourth Born's thinking process.

When Onlies and Fourth Borns discuss something, they begin and end at opposite ends of the spectrum. Let's say an Only woman and a Fourth Born man are talking about opening a Christmas Club account at their bank. The Only looks forward to December, when they will have a cache of money to spend on the holidays without having to dip into their regular savings account. The Fourth Born wonders what will happen if they need that money before Christmas, and whether they might get a better interest rate if they just put the money in a short-term CD. After discussing it, the Fourth Born says the Christmas Club idea sounds pretty good. The Only, taking the Fourth Born's comment as a conclusion, goes to the bank the next day and sets up the account. But when she tells the Fourth Born what she did, he gets upset because, on thinking it over, he really would rather put some money in a CD. The Only, having organized her thinking around what he said yesterday, says, "But you told me that this was a good idea." The Fourth Born feels trapped and may react with anger. The Only feels confused and guilty, so she reorganizes her thinking around the Fourth Born's latest statement. In the meantime, the Fourth Born has been analyzing her reaction and has decided that the Christmas Club account is a good idea after all, thinking this will satisfy the Only. But when he tells her of his new conclusion, the Only is thrown off balance again because she has already reorganized herself to accept the CD option. This cycle can go on and on, building frustration in the Only and anger in the Fourth Born.

The Only's need to be organized can give rise to feelings of immaturity in the Fourth Born. For instance, Onlies tend to like cellular phones because these provide an additional way to keep track of their partners so they can organize their time. Onlies like to know when to expect their partners' arrival home, and they definitely want some warning if their partners are likely to be early or late. But to the Fourth Born, this type of "checking up and checking in" feels like the bad old days when Mom always had to keep track of the children. In the Fourth Born's mind, mature people do not check in with their partners, and they don't allow their partners to keep track of them.

The cycle of Only organizing and Fourth Born analyzing can be broken when an Only stands his or her ground in the relationship. One couple, an Only woman and a Fourth Born man, had been very happily married for twenty years and still held hands while they walked. Clearly they had learned how to enjoy each other, despite their differences. When asked the secret to their happiness, the woman answered, "I'm hard to live with." She meant that she often insisted on having her own way. Her Fourth Born husband could analyze what she said, and when he talked to her again about the same subject, she held the same stance she had held before. This gave him a sense of security; he didn't have to start analyzing again because her stance was the same. This woman also helped her Fourth Born husband feel mature by standing up to him. Onlies who continually give in to Fourth Borns can create feelings of anger; to Fourth Borns, such acquiescence feels condescending, as though they are being treated like children. Standing up to Fourth Borns helps them feel grown-up, because this kind of conflict fits in with their idea that you have to work hard in life.

Fourth Born men and women can be abusive to their partners, too. One Fourth Born woman beat up on her Only boyfriend. When he told her in no uncertain terms that he wouldn't put up with that behavior, and then backed up his statement by breaking up with her, she did everything she could to get back together with him. Although they still had conflict in their relationship, she never beat up on him again; he made her feel mature by refusing to take her abuse.

EXERCISE: Onlies like to make decisions quickly so they don't have to worry about them any more. Fourth Borns like to take their time in making decisions so they won't be trapped by a bad decision. If you're a Fourth Born, you can help your Only partner accept your need to wait by saying, "Let me think about this." It is helpful if you can give a time when you expect to make a decision—"Let me think about this for a couple of days," for example—because the Only can get organized to wait for a specific time.

If you're an Only, you can encourage your Fourth Born partner to set a time for making a decision by saying, "Can you help me make a decision by Friday?" By turning it into a challenge, you help the Fourth Born feel mature, and by setting a deadline, you give the Fourth Born time and yourself a schedule.

The adult Only Child's coping mechanisms were developed from his unique challenges as a child—the need to play alone without feeling lonely and the need to minimize intrusion by others. First Borns have a different set of childhood challenges and a different set of coping mechanisms, which we explore in the next chapter.

CHAPTER FOUR

The First Born

First Borns are the Rodney Dangerfields of the world. They're always looking for respect, and they can get terribly unhappy when they don't find it—especially when they substitute respect, admiration or approval for love.

This is quite common among First Borns because, from their point of view, there is no love in the world. For them, love disappeared when the new baby came along and captured all of Mom and Dad's affection. And if there isn't any love, then the only things left for First Borns to seek are respect, admiration and approval.

Typically, First Borns will seek respect at home; they look for admiration and approval from the outside world. Respect means agreement and obedience from spouses and children. Disagreement, especially from their partners, can be intolerable to First Borns because to them it feels like the failure of love. First Borns who feel this way can feel compelled to convince their partners to think as they do, no matter what. Away from home, First Borns want to impress others to earn admiration and approval; these mean the First Born has been able to please a boss, coworkers or clients.

First Borns tend to be out of touch with themselves, and they have difficulty establishing connections with other people. Because they usually are the eldest children, First Borns didn't have to understand their younger siblings to get through childhood; they could just over-power brothers and sisters when they needed to. As adults, First Borns still tend to use power to influence others' behavior, often in the form of an ultimatum such as, "Do what I say or I'm leaving." They can be in for a rude awakening when their partners call their bluff.

Making the initial emotional connection with a First Born isn't easy, and keeping that connection going can be even tougher. But it helps to understand the First Born's unique view of the world.

EXERCISE: Imagine yourself at three years old. Mom and Dad have brought home a new baby, but, even though they explained that you were going to have a new little brother or sister, you don't really understand. All you know is that this baby, a stranger, now gets all the attention. Mom sits you on the couch and tells you to wait while she goes off and does things with the baby, and all the time Mom is smiling, laughing and making cooing sounds to the baby. She doesn't coo to you; in fact, if you try to get her attention, she responds sternly, making it clear to you that the baby comes first. You don't know what you did to lose your parents' love, but you're sure you must have done something wrong; otherwise, why would they want a new baby? You decide you must not risk losing any more of Mom and Dad's love, so you begin to behave like a guest in your own home, fearful of expressing a need, a want or an objection, lest Mom and Dad love you even less. When you can feel the discomfort and fear this scenario evokes, you are imagining what it feels like to be a First Born.

What Did I Do?

First Borns often feel guilty, especially if they think they've offended someone else. These feelings go way back to when the new baby came into the First Born's home and stole the parental limelight. Until that baby showed up, the First Born was really an Only Child, the center of

Mom and Dad's universe. As an Only, this child sometimes felt smoth-ered because there was no one else around to distract the parents; there was too much love. Then, without any warning, this strange infant comes along and suddenly the older child is no longer in the limelight—he's been pushed off to wait in the wings while the baby soaks up all the attention. Practically overnight, the First Born goes from a world with too much love to a world without any love at all. The First Born is convinced that he or she must have done something horribly wrong to make Mom and Dad withdraw their love.

Imagine reliving that kind of heart-rending loss over and over for a lifetime. This is what happens for many First Borns. Adult First Borns most likely won't be able to identify the source of their guilt, although they may be aware that they often feel guilty. If someone around them is unhappy, First Borns will agonize over whether they are the cause of the unhappiness. If they turn down a request, even an unreasonable one, First Borns will feel guilty, thinking others will dislike them for saying, "No." If they take a sick day, they'll feel guilty, believing their co-workers will think less of them for it. And on those rare occasions when First Borns speak their minds or express their needs, they'll feel guilty for being selfish or self-indulgent—qualities others can't possibly like or approve of, in the First Born view.

To other birth orders, it can look as though First Borns are far too outer-directed, taking responsibility for others' feelings even when they don't need to. To First Borns, guilt is an internal regulator that keeps them from offending other people, which could lead to more loss of affection.

EXERCISE: Most people feel guilty when they've done something wrong; First Borns feel guilty even when they haven't done anything wrong. It's a habit that First Borns fell into at a very young age, and it can be a very difficult habit to kick. This exercise is designed to help the First Born think about his or her feelings of guilt from a more objective point of view.

Make three columns on a sheet of paper. Title the first column "Actions," the second column "Why," and the third column "Does it matter?" In the first column, write down things you've done or said that made you feel guilty—deciding not to fold the laundry, for example, or being short-tempered with the telemarketer who called during dinner. In the second column, write down why you felt guilty about the item in the first column—your husband was irritated that his shirt was wrinkled; the telemarketer sounded offended. In the third column, write "yes" or "no" and the reason for choosing "yes" or "no." For example, if your husband simply wore a different shirt, you would put "no" in the third column for that item. If your husband didn't have another shirt to wear, and he was late because you or he had to iron the wrinkled shirt, your answer to "Does it matter?" might be "yes."

Note: Many First Borns may feel guilty about putting "no" in the "Does it matter?" column because they've learned throughout their lives to let everything matter, and this can also be a difficult habit to break. Writing down the actions you feel guilty about and the reasons you feel guilty about them will help you identify specific causes for your feelings of guilt, and making the determination of whether it matters will help you discover times when you can let go of those feelings. The more often you do this exercise, the easier it will become to identify times when the honest answer to "Does it matter?" is "no." And that is the beginning of the end for your habitual cycle of guilt.

You Go First

There is no such thing as enduring unconditional love for First Borns. They risk losing love—or respect, admiration or approval—every time they express an opinion, articulate an idea or state a preference. So, often, they just don't do it. Instead, they tend to go along with someone else's suggestions, and they get so good at doing this that, many times, First Borns honestly don't have any idea what they think, feel or believe.

First Borns are research thinkers. They don't know what they think until they find out what someone else thinks. The First Born's favorite phrase is, "I don't know," and First Borns often will say they don't know even when they do know. In conversation, the First Born will look at you when you're talking and likely will nod in agreement or raise the eyebrows in an unspoken invitation for you to continue. When the First Born is speaking, he or she typically will avoid eye contact with you and may use a lot of verbal "fillers"—"ahs," "ers" and "ums" between phrases.

As part of a group, the First Born will sit back and watch to find out what the majority thinks, and then most likely will go along with the majority. As leaders, First Borns may ask others what they think, but in the end they will expect everyone to agree with them.

EXERCISE: Writing can be a very effective tool to help First Borns sort out their thoughts and feelings. First Borns tend to gloss over their own thoughts, as if they were driving extremely fast down a highway, so that everything around them is blurred. Writing is like stopping the car, getting out, and walking. The slower pace allows you to become aware of many more things.

When you write, begin with the knowledge that you are going to immediately destroy what you have written. No one else is going to read it, so you don't have to worry about what anyone else will think about your subject, your writing style or even spelling and punctuation. The purpose of writing is to help you explore your own thoughts—even those that you might not want to share with anyone else.

Write about whatever comes to mind in whatever order it comes to you, and write for as long as you need to until your thoughts become clear to you. Do this exercise whenever you feel confused or out of touch with how you really feel about something.

I'll Give You a Hint

Because First Borns are so concerned about offending others, they find it virtually impossible to come out and say what they want. Even a simple question like, "Do you want to go out to eat tonight?" is apt to evoke an "I don't know" from the First Born. If a First Born really does want to go out to eat, he or she won't just come out and say, "I want to go out to eat." Instead, First Borns will hint at what they want, perhaps saying something like this: "We haven't tried that new Italian place yet." Hinting gives the First Born room to back away from an opinion or preference if the other person appears hostile, or even indifferent, to the hint. Suppose the First Born's partner says, "I've heard that new Italian place isn't very good." The First Born hasn't actually committed to going to that restaurant and can counter with, "Oh. Well, how about Chinese?"

Hinting also gives the First Born lots of room to compromise. First Borns are good at this because they are so intent on not offending anyone. If the partner wants steak and the First Born is in the mood for pasta, the First Born will suggest a restaurant that serves both.

Hints and the common "I don't know. What do you think?" response from the First Born can be a source of frustration for other birth order personalities. Each birth order has its own way of trying to please a partner, but First Borns make it difficult for anyone to please them because they can't communicate what they want. It takes a lot of practice for First Borns to learn how to say what they think and feel without being overwhelmed by guilt. And when First Borns do master this hard-earned ability, it can be quite an adjustment for those around them, who aren't accustomed to hearing strong opinions from the First Born.

EXERCISE: The phrase "I don't know" tends to close the communication door because when we say those words, others assume that we don't want to talk about it. "I don't know" is a stock response, requiring no time for thought; real answers require time for thought.

To build your own awareness of saying "I don't know," ask your partner to flag that phrase in your conversations and respond with, "Take your time." This will alert you to think about what you do know and formulate an answer. By telling you to take your time, your partner is showing he or she is willing to wait for an answer.

With practice, First Borns can learn to be more in touch with what they think and feel and, as that connection grows, the words "I don't know" will gradually fade out of the First Born's vocabulary.

All I Have to Do Is Dream

First Borns are always chasing approval and admiration, hoping to impress those around them. In their daydreams, First Borns envision great accomplishments and bask in the pleasurable glow of anticipated accolades. They see themselves back in their rightful place in the limelight, the center of attention, a role model for others to look up to and emulate.

This kind of daydreaming is the First Born's particular way of procrastinating. It provides an escape from the mundane chores of the here and now, which may provide little opportunity for the admiration the First Born seeks. This also stems from those first days with the new baby brother or sister. Back then, the First Born had to wait for Mom and Dad to take care of the baby; then it would be the First Born's turn to get some attention. The First Born learned to look forward to a pleasant future and ignore the present.

Some First Borns figure out that channeling some of their dreaming energy into today's tasks helps them eventually realize their ambitions; these are the First Borns who climb the corporate ladder from sales representative to CEO, whose political careers start at City Hall and end at the White House. Others will continue to dream and talk about their dreams, but their loved ones may become frustrated with the First Born's lack of follow-through.

EXERCISE: Although daydreaming of future accomplishments is a typical First Born trait, all birth orders can benefit from this "here and now" exercise. This exercise has two components. First, flag the "someday" concept in conversation with your partner. Whenever either of you says, "Someday, I'd like to…" or any variation ("I've always wanted to …," "I wonder whether I could …," etc.), the other responds with, "That sounds good. What do you like about things right now?" Saying "I don't know" is not allowed (see previous exercise). Focus on the present and the pleasant things in your life at the moment. Telling your partner what you like about your life right now helps you recognize that good things are not out of reach for you, and that recognition allows you to enjoy those good things.

The other part of this exercise involves talking about those dreams for the future. When either of you brings up a goal or dream, the other partner asks questions to prompt definitive thinking—not just day-dreaming—about that goal or dream. Questions that promote this type of thinking include "How would you go about doing that?," "What kinds of skills would you need to do that?" and "How have other people done this?" By talking in terms of "how" and "what," you focus on the journey rather than the destination (the goal or dream). That helps you decide whether the destination is worth the effort it would take to get there—or whether you'd rather concentrate your energy on a different destination.

The First Born and the Only Child

Although most, if not all, First Borns started life with an Only Child Birth Order Personality, First Borns don't really understand Onlies. On the other hand, the Only doesn't understand the First Born, either—a definite plus from the First Born's point of view, because, without that understanding, the Only can't dethrone the First Born the way other birth orders can.

First Borns find Onlies attractive because Onlies provide fodder for the First Borns' research thinking. The First Born wants to know what the Only is thinking and feeling; the Only freely expresses emotions and opinions, so the First Born gets the answers he or she needs. If the First Born is male, he gets the information he needs from the Only to find direction. If the First Born is female, she gets the information she needs to relate to the Only on Only Child terms.

Still, First Borns and Onlies can run into difficulties, especially when it comes to communicating. Onlies tend to project their own thoughts and feelings onto others, and that's particularly easy to do with First Borns, who aren't in touch with themselves and don't know what they think and feel. First Borns, who don't want to offend anyone for fear of losing the other's love or esteem, can go overboard in accommodating the Only's need for order and time alone. Many times, First Borns act like guests in their own homes, walking around on egg shells to avoid offending their partners.

Carol, a First Born, fell into this pattern with Ray, an Only. Carol picked up on Ray's typically Only slogan—"Leave me alone. I'll do it myself" —and responded by focusing on their children rather than relating to Ray. She didn't realize that Ray just wanted some time to himself, not all the time to himself. When he complained about her devoting all her time to the children, Carol felt guilty, but she didn't know what to do to please Ray. Without knowing it, Ray was still sending out signals that he wanted to be left alone to do his own thing. Carol, given no other cues to follow, acted on those signals. The result: These two didn't connect much at all, and in the end their relationship just dried up for lack of connection.

EXERCISE: First Borns are wont to use superlatives as they try to impress others. They describe things as being the best, the strongest, the worst, the ugliest, and so on. But Onlies tend to attach their own meanings to a First Born's words, so without real description from the First Born, communication between these two birth orders can get mangled in short order.

To counter this effect, practice using description in place of superlatives. For instance, instead of saying, "I've never seen anything like it," you can say, "That's different from what I expected," and then go on to describe what was different.

Try translating the following general superlatives into real description. Test yourself with your partner by asking him or her which one is more likely to keep his or her attention.

- I really like that.
- That's the hardest thing I have done.
- I am most impressed with what you did.
- I am really bothered by that.
- You are the greatest.

- That is unbelievable.
- He is the funniest person I know.

Add some of your own favorite superlatives to this list (ask your partner if you're not sure which words you use the most) and translate them into description.

The First Born and Other First Borns

This pairing is extraordinarily rare for a number of reasons. First, two First Borns will try to impress each other rather than connect with each other. Second, each will look to the other for clues on what to think, say and do, but neither will give those clues. Third, being unable to figure each other out or open up to each other, two First Borns will be bored by each other.

Some of you read that last paragraph and are saying to yourselves, "Wait a minute—I know lots of couples where both are First Borns." And you may be right. Usually, though, we find that, even in couples where both partners are the oldest children in their families, only one of them has a First Born Birth Order Personality—and often neither of them does. Remember, psychological birth order is not necessarily the same as chronological birth order. First Borns and all the other birth order personalities can develop at any chronological place in the family; psychological birth order is determined by individual circumstances during childhood, not by accidents of timing.

That said, there certainly are cases, though rare, of two First Borns getting together. When they do, they have a terrible time connecting. Each wants the other's approval and respect, but neither is very comfortable with giving approval and respect. There tends to be a fundamental imbalance, a lack of give and take, between two First Borns. Special circumstances, including alcohol and drug use, can mask that imbalance well enough to encourage two First Borns to pursue a relationship.

Matt and Denise, both First Borns, began their relationship when they were using drugs. Matt had misgivings at the wedding; his counselor at the time had even warned him against marrying Denise, but he went through with it anyway. They managed all right for the first four or five years, but things went downhill quickly as they began demanding more and more respect from each other instead of trying to make each other feel loved. Because they were out of touch with themselves, they couldn't tell each other what they wanted and needed. They could only look for their substitutes for love—respect, admiration, approval—from each other, and neither was able to give enough to the other. After several separations and several failed attempts at reconciliation, Matt and Denise finally went their separate ways.

EXERCISE: Instead of seeking respect from each other, First Borns can focus on making each other feel loved. One of the easiest ways to do this is with the phrase, "I love you because you're you." This is especially effective when your partner has accomplished something special or important—a promotion at work, a woodworking project, anything likely to garner admiration or approval. By saying, "That's wonderful, honey, but I love you because you're you," you let your partner know that your feelings for him or her are not conditioned on accomplishments or accolades. And that unconditional love is really what the First Born is seeking.

The First Born and the Second Born

First Borns and Second Borns don't seem to be naturally drawn to each other very often. The Second Born, who had to figure out First Borns as a child, can see through the First Born's attempts to impress and is able to dethrone the First Born without thinking twice about it. This makes the Second Born a little scary to the First Born. When these two birth orders do get together, the marriage can be stable but might also be a little awkward.

The Second Born's dry, teasing sense of humor and criticism can be very wearing on a First Born. Helen, a First Born, took her husband's Second Born teasing seriously, thinking it provided a clue for her to be able to please him. She began to feel that she couldn't do anything well enough to suit him, and eventually she stopped having any opinions of her own and began apologizing continually for whatever she did. Gene, her husband, became frustrated because he couldn't have the give-and-take conversations he would have liked to have with Helen; she was so careful not to give him any reason to find fault with her that she literally could not communicate with him. Helen sunk into a depression and went on anti-depressants, which only made things worse because they dulled her mind. As she tried harder and harder to "make Gene happy," Gene became more and more frustrated, and eventually they divorced.

Fred and Nancy were able to get closer than many First Born/Second Born couples, but only after years of unhappiness. Fred, the Second Born, had grown up in a family where his father was gone much of the time and he was left alone; close relationships were alien to him. Nancy, the First Born, felt safe to Fred. She didn't have strong opinions, she wasn't demanding, and she went along with whatever Fred wanted. Although not strongly drawn to each other, they dated for a very long time and finally got married because it seemed the thing to do.

Problems in their relationship cropped up when Fred found a career that kept him away from home for extended periods. He insisted that Nancy have a life of her own, suggesting things she could do in the community or with her friends rather than sitting home alone pining for him. He provided well for her, but he affirmed his "loner" personality in choosing this course, and Nancy felt unloved. She interpreted Fred's "loner" identity as meaning that he did not need her. As she became more unhappy, she became more critical of him, while he expressed his feelings indirectly by becoming more fatalistic. It wasn't until they learned about birth order that they were able to understand each other and, very important for a healthy relationship, find humor in each other's attitudes, behaviors, and even feelings. For the first time, this understanding allowed them to be drawn closer together and become comfortable with each other.

Some First Borns and Second Borns are able to forge a strong bond that lasts a lifetime. Hannah and Don had such a relationship. Hannah, the First Born, was more independent than many First Borns, which made her less apt to overdo her attempts to please Don. Don was less inclined to tease than many Second Borns, which made him less critical of Hannah. They both worked at jobs they enjoyed; they agreed on lifestyle issues; they both believed in following rules and frugal living. Although their relationship seemed at times to be more formal than many marriages, they cared deeply about each other and were able to lead full lives from the stable foundation they built together.

EXERCISE: The Second Born's correction, though not meant this way, feels like disapproval to the First Born—and disapproval feels like yet another failure of love. First Borns can counter the Second Born's correction by saying, "This may not be perfect, but…" However, many First Borns may be averse to such directness.

If you find yourself unable to come right out and say that something doesn't have to be perfect, try this approach: Use the writing exercise provided earlier in this chapter to figure out what you think about a specific correction or criticism your partner made. When you're done, destroy the writing. If you decide to talk to your partner about this specific thing, say, "I've thought about this, and I know it's not perfect, but…" This lets your partner know both that perfection is not a requirement and that your comments are the result of reflection, not a knee-jerk reaction to the correction or criticism.

The First Born and the Third Born

This may be the most compatible match for First Borns, particularly if the Third Born is a fearful type (one with a Second Born sibling of the opposite sex). The fearful Third Born doesn't challenge the First Born the way other birth orders do. This Third Born is compassionate, gentle, and communicative. He or she appreciates the First Born, which makes the First Born feel good; respect, admiration, and approval seem to flow naturally from the fearful Third Born, so the First Born feels comfortable. The First Born feels safe for the Third Born because there isn't as much pressure to please someone who doesn't know what he or she thinks, wants or feels.

The big hurdle in this relationship can be boredom, especially for the First Born. A steady diet of respect, admiration, and approval is like eating nothing but sweet pastries; after a while, you start looking around for something else. One First Born man had an apparently idyllic marriage with his Third Born wife, until he met another, more assertive woman. The change was a challenge for this man, though no one else understood why he left his wife.

First Borns and fearless Third Borns (ones with Second Born siblings of the same sex) have a much tougher time. The fearless Third Born tends to be more aggressive and more demanding of his or her partner. But First Borns can be drawn to this type of Third Born, especially the Third Born's sense of humor. Jeff, a First Born, enjoyed the put-down quality of Robin's humor when they were dating. In a strange sort of way, Jeff felt Robin was showing him respect when she poked fun at him; she used her Third Born sense of humor to show that she knew Jeff could take a joke. As their relationship progressed, Robin took the lead, even in proposing marriage. Decisions were made according to her preference rather than his; Jeff felt comfortable because he could go along with what she wanted and didn't have to decide what he wanted. Their marriage continued because Jeff felt challenged enough by Robin's aggressive ways, and Robin felt safe with Jeff's accommodating ways.

EXERCISE: First Borns tend to do things not out of any enthusiasm for the tasks, but just to get them done. Their reward is a sense of relief when a task is done. In this mindset, everything becomes a chore and there is no satisfaction—only the absence of pressure—in completing something. When it comes to doing things for their partners, First Borns can easily lose sight of the satisfaction most of us feel when we do good things for someone else. This exercise is designed to help the First Born find that feeling of satisfaction.

With your partner, make a list of the things you do for each other. This isn't a competition to see who does more; this is a way to remind yourselves of the good things you do for each other. Help each other complete the list by suggesting things to include, and remember that the bulk of your list will be made up of small things—preparing the coffee pot at night so all your partner has to do in the morning is turn it on, making sure the car is full of gas, taking out the trash, and so on. In a relationship, these little things we do every day carry far more weight than the big things we do once in a great while.

To feel genuine satisfaction in these little things, we must be able to enjoy doing them and enjoy having them done for us. If you or your partner feels awkward accepting the things you do for each other, discussing this awkwardness can help you determine whether the discomfort lies in the way these things are done or in the recipient's difficulty in accepting the good things that are done for him or her.

The First Born and the Fourth Born

This is another not-too-common birth order combination. Fourth Borns who are super-mature are much too direct, insightful, and aggressive for the First Born's comfort. Immature Fourth Borns—those with a childlike quality in their personalities—are more likely to appeal to the First Born, although such relationships often are initiated by the Fourth Born. In these cases, the First Born feels good because the Fourth Born is playful, non-aggressive, and responsive to the First Born. The First Born tends to agree with the Fourth Born, so they do things the Fourth Born wants to do.

Problems can arise when the Fourth Born challenges the First Born. When this happens, the First Born often will be at a loss. Often, a Fourth Born challenges others because he or she wants to feel grown-up, but in order to feel grown-up, the Fourth Born needs the other person to stand his or her ground. First Borns aren't good at standing their ground because to do so might offend the other person. When challenged by a Fourth Born, the First Born, who wants to please, is unable to return the challenge and is utterly at sea when the Fourth Born becomes frustrated with his or her acquiescence.

This is what happened with Tom and Brenda. Brenda, the Fourth Born, had taken the initiative throughout their courtship. Tom, the First Born, went along with Brenda because he didn't know what he wanted to do. He was never completely sure of the relationship, but Brenda seemed to be sure, so he followed her lead and, in this spirit, they got married. They seemed to get along well for several years, but Brenda became increasingly unhappy because Tom never challenged her. Without his challenge, Brenda couldn't feel mature; even when she challenged him, he just backed down. The relationship ended eventually without any emotional fireworks. Brenda, who had initiated the marriage, also initiated the break up.

Had Tom been more in touch with himself and better able to express his thoughts and feelings, Brenda might not have become so unhappy. If he had expressed a strong opinion about something now and then, especially one that disagreed with hers, she would have been able to feel grown-up, and Tom might have been able to feel more secure in the relationship.

EXERCISE: First Borns have a hard time understanding that other birth orders—particularly Fourth Borns—want them to disagree occasionally. For the Fourth Born, disagreement is a challenge that helps the Fourth Born feel mature. But for the First Born, disagreement is anathema to approval, admiration, and respect, and many First Borns will feel guilty about expressing an opinion that might offend their partners.

Fourth Borns (and other birth orders) can counter this First Born tendency by saying, "You might not agree with this, but. . ." This phrase tells the First Born that he or she is not required, or even expected, to agree with you. With this sort of passive permission to disagree, the First Born's automatic agreement is turned off, and he or she can then make an active decision about agreeing.

First Borns who disagree with their Fourth Born partners can elicit this passive permission to disagree by saying, "Can we disagree on this?" This phrasing makes disagreeing a challenge, which the Fourth Born needs, without turning the disagreement into a confrontation.

For First Borns to learn to listen to themselves, to feel comfortable expressing their opinions, and to let go of their feelings of guilt, they have to be able to accept that they are lovable for who they are, not for what they do. Second Borns, on the other hand, believe deep down that they are worthy of love only if they can achieve perfection—an impossible standard for anyone, but one the Second Born keeps chasing nevertheless. We take a detailed look at the Second Born personality in the next chapter.

CHAPTER FIVE

The Second Born

Perhaps you've seen this commercial. Two twenty-something guys sit on a couch, watching television. "Want a cold one?" the host asks his guest.

"Yeah," the guest replies, his eyes glued on the television screen.

The host reaches over his head, grasps a chain, and gives it a sharp tug. The guest disappears under approximately eight feet of snow.

"Cold enough for ya?" the host asks with a smirk.

"Well, it's cold," admits the guest, blowing snow off his upper lip. "But it's not Coors Light."

That's a Second Born for you.

We all know people like this guy—people for whom good is never quite good enough, people who, even while admitting that something is better than they expected, still somehow manage to find fault. Getting a compliment from these people—a real compliment, with no "ifs," no "ands" and especially no "buts"—is like winning the Boston Marathon: It happens, but not very often, and not to very many of us.

The thing is, there's generally no malice behind a Second Born's criticisms. The guy in the beer commercial wasn't being mean; he was simply pointing out how "cold" could be better.

NASCAR Winston Cup Driver Terry Labonte is another classic Second Born. His 2001 race-day commercials, featuring his criticisms of everything from a fingerprint on the windshield to the blueness of Tony the Tiger's nose on the hood of his Chevrolet Monte Carlo, demonstrate the Second Born's relentless pursuit of perfection.

One man whose wife was a Second Born had learned to understand her need for perfection. When the couple decided to wallpaper a room in their house, the man got up on the ladder to put the paper up, while his wife acted as support staff on the floor. The man was doing a good job, making sure the paper was straight and smoothing out air pockets as he affixed it to the wall. But from his wife's perspective, he wasn't doing it right. She became increasingly antsy and frustrated as she watched him, and finally she threw up her hands and told him to get off the ladder. She climbed up herself, muttering criticisms about the incompetence of men in general and her husband in particular, who, in her view at that moment, never could do anything right.

You might expect the man to be hurt, defensive, angry. But while his wife was up on the ladder, adjusting the paper just so against the corner, the man turned to a friend who had been present during the whole scene, smiled and winked. He understood his wife's need for perfection; he knew her criticisms came from this need; and he was able to let her vent without taking it personally.

If you don't understand how this birth order thinks, feels, and communicates, home life with your Second Born partner can be challenging at best and utterly heartrending at worst.

EXERCISE: Imagine you are two years old. You have just discovered that you can create colorful lines on paper using crayons. This is such a thrilling discovery that you can't wait to show Mom. Your older brother has been coloring, too, watching you while he creates his own drawing—a picture, not just a collection of colorful lines. Just as you go to show Mom your drawing, your brother gets ahead of you and shows Mom his picture. Mom compliments him, then she looks at your drawing and compliments you, too. But the difference between your drawing and your brother's is obvious, so you don't believe Mom's compliment to you is genuine. You go off, ashamed of your pathetic attempt at drawing and resolving someday to do something perfectly.

When you can feel the overwhelming sense of inadequacy of this young child, you are experiencing what it feels like to be a Second Born.

Good, Better, Best

The perfection-seeking side of the Second Born has many manifestations. It influences their thinking patterns: Second Borns think by evaluating, looking for pitfalls that can interfere with the pursuit of perfection. It influences their choices: Second Borns are drawn to projects rather than goals. Projects are specific and clearly defined, with step-by-step needs, so perfection is attainable. Goals are more tenuous; there may be many ways to reach a goal, so "the right way," or perfection, is not attainable.

Second Borns expect perfection from others. They offer correction instead of compliments, pointing out how something can be done better by saying, "You need to. . ." In extreme cases, Second Borns view their loved ones not as individual human beings, but as projects to be perfected.

Second Borns are always chasing perfection in some area, but not in all areas. The Second Born's desk at work might be almost sterile in its neatness and organization, but his kitchen at home might look like the last days of Pompeii. A Second Born aspiring musician will start over if she makes a mistake playing Chopin on the piano, but she'll ignore a missing button on her blouse.

This pursuit of perfection makes it difficult for the Second Born to give or receive compliments. When the Second Born was a child, his or her older sibling usually got the compliments, and that hurt the Second Born's feelings. As an adult, the Second Born doesn't want to cause that hurt in anyone else, so he or she will simply refrain from giving praise. Instead, the Second Born is more likely to point out mistakes, operating from the assumption that other people share the

Second Born's need to "do better." Unless it is pointed out to them, Second Borns usually aren't aware that their continual correcting can cause bad feelings in others.

On the other hand, when someone offers a compliment to the Second Born, the Second Born often feels uncomfortable, and as a result, he or she may feel compelled to point out flaws the other has missed. If you compliment a Second Born on his suit or on the report she wrote, he will reply by telling you the suit was off-the-rack, and she will say she didn't have enough time to do the report the way she wanted to. It takes a lot of practice for Second Borns to learn how to accept compliments graciously. One woman who was aware of her penchant for dismissing compliments trained herself to say, "Thank you," and then she would nibble on the inside of her lower lip to keep herself from saying anything else. Even so, this woman still feels genuinely surprised when she receives a compliment, and in her heart of hearts she believes the people who compliment her are too easily impressed.

EXERCISE: Second Borns naturally look for flaws in just about everything. To look for what's right instead of what's wrong, say three positive things before you can say one negative or critical thing. Make this a rule for everyone in your household, and ask your partner to help you enforce it. It will take a bit of practice, but after a while you'll notice that the critical, flaw-seeking part of you (or your partner) won't have quite the same edge.

Anything You Can Do . . .
When the perfection-pursuing part of the Second Born's personality is engaged, he or she can be highly competitive, eager to prove his or her ability to do it right and better than anyone else. And if they can't do it right or better than someone else, Second Borns can suffer agonizing feelings of inadequacy.

Madeleine was a classic competitive Second Born. She was the valedictorian and president of her high school class; she ran many student organizations and became the highest-ranked female high school debater in her state. She met her future husband at a debate; he was the highest-ranked male high school debater in the state. After their wedding, Madeleine entered a career in banking; the details involved in the field appealed to her Second Born personality. Because she was so involved in high school, she attended every class reunion—that is, until she and her husband divorced. Although she remarried a couple of years later and has been successful in her career, Madeleine hasn't been to a high school reunion since her divorce. To her competitive nature, the failure of her first marriage is unacceptable, and she cannot face her former classmates with that failure hanging over her.

Sometimes, a Second Born's feelings of inadequacy paradoxically yield a fear of success. When Second Borns do something well, they might feel they owe their success to luck rather than skill, and they don't feel confident in their ability to do well again. They learn to avoid situations where others might expect too much of them; if, for example, a Second Born is offered a promotion at work, she might turn it down because she's afraid she'll fail at a higher level.

Andy, a Second Born man, made his family's life very difficult because of his fear of success. He worked at a small food processing plant, and he was very good at his job—so good that his superiors wanted to move him into a management position. Instead of accepting the promotion, Andy decided that he really wanted to work with sporting goods, not food. So he quit his job at the plant and got an entry-level job filling orders for a sporting goods distributor. Again, he did a very good job, and the distributor wanted to make Andy head of the shipping department. But Andy decided he really wanted to work outdoors, so he quit and got a job as a lineman for a utility company. Naturally, he did a good job there, too, and he was about to be made foreman when he decided that what he really wanted was to live near the mountains, so he quit his job, moved his family out West and took yet another entry-level position in yet another field.

EXERCISE: Although Second Borns often feel inadequate, they seldom admit to it because inadequacy is really imperfection. But those feelings of inadequacy can be turned to the Second Born's advantage when approached in the right way.

The most common objection Second Borns raise when they feel inadequate is, "I don't know how to do this." By turning this objection into a question—"How do I do this?"—the source of inadequacy becomes instead a project and therefore something the Second Born can accomplish. Partners can help their Second Born mates work through their inadequacy by turning objections into questions and by expressing confidence in the Second Born's ability.

Tell Me More, Tell Me More

Second Borns are detail-oriented, because perfection—or the lack of it—is in the details. They read the fine print on everything: insurance policies, loan applications, nutrition labels. They drive salesmen crazy because they always read the entire contract before they sign it, and heaven help you if there's a typo in there somewhere.

Check out the paragraph about Terry Labonte again. The fact that we told you he drives a Chevrolet Monte Carlo is a pretty good tip-off that at least one of us is a Second Born; other birth order personalities might be content with a simple word like "car," but a Second Born would never be satisfied with such a generic term.

This craving for details caused problems in Mark and Susan's marriage. Susan was a Second Born and wanted to know everything about Mark's day; Mark was satisfied with the bottom line—it was a good day, or it wasn't a good day—and didn't see any need to go into details. In fact, since he worked in a factory, he felt there wasn't much detail to go into, anyway.

Susan felt Mark's refusal to share details meant he didn't care enough to let her know what was going on with his work life. For her, it was a major breakdown in communication, and she became more and more unhappy.

Mark didn't understand Susan's feelings, but when he was told about her need for details, he decided to try to satisfy that need. He began making notes to himself about things that happened at work, things he heard from his coworkers, anything he could think of that Susan might be interested in when he got home. He'd review the notes on the way home so he'd be ready to talk with her when he walked in the door.

When she asked him how his day was, he still began with the bottom line—it was good, it wasn't good. But then he would tell her the things he'd heard and the things that happened. Susan lapped it up like a cat with a saucer of cream. The communication lines were open again, Susan felt like Mark wanted to include her in all aspects of his life, and their relationship has been the stronger for it ever since.

EXERCISE: Details are almost always important to Second Borns, but they aren't always relevant. You can satisfy your Second Born partner's need for details by following Mark's example and making notes about your day to share when you get home. You also can help your Second Born partner step back from his or her detail-orientation by saying, "I want to look at/talk about the big picture right now." This lets the Second Born refocus his or her mental energy and stay on track with you; at the same time, it reassures the Second Born that there will be a time for details later.

The Spock Syndrome

Remember Mr. Spock from the original Star Trek? He embraced the logical side of his Vulcan ancestry and used that logic to keep an extraordinarily tight rein on his human, feeling side. Once in a while, Spock would let his guard down and display emotion, but such episodes were rare and he always recovered his logical control quickly.

If he weren't an alien, Spock would be a Second Born. Second Borns don't like feelings much; logic is so much cleaner, so much safer. They learned early on that feelings can hurt, so they learned to suppress them. They're so good at this that oftentimes they aren't even aware of their own feelings, much less able to explain them to someone else. Because they suppress their emotions, Second Borns are the most likely of any of the birth orders to break into uncontrollable sobbing—and often they won't even be able to tell you why. It's simply the build-up of emotion that has had no other outlet; like steam under pressure, it can build for only so long before something bursts.

On the other hand, Second Borns are highly sensitive to others' feelings, especially feelings of tension and anger. When Second Borns sense these, they will use their considerable peacemaking skills to diffuse tension and bring things back to an even keel.

That's not to say Second Borns are always thinking about how other people feel; they aren't, simply because they prefer not to think about feelings at all. But because they have this sensitivity, Second Borns can display great empathy and understanding when they are reminded to think about how other people feel. For example, one woman who was having emotional problems received little compassion from her Second Born manager when these problems affected her work. The manager, frustrated by the employee's poor performance (and apparent lack of interest in doing better), came down pretty hard on this worker until another manager took him to task and said, "Think about how this woman feels." As the story of the employee's troubles unfolded, tears came to the Second Born manager's eyes; he was able to empathize and to demonstrate the compassion the woman needed to help her through her problems at work.

EXERCISE: Most Second Borns find it much easier to write about their feelings than to talk about them. To get in touch with your feelings, set aside at least one hour a week to write about yourself. You can do this in the form of a journal or diary, or you can just fill up a blank page on a notepad or a computer screen. Write about what has happened to you in the last week, how those happenings made you feel, and how you think other people felt about those happenings. This is a private time for you to indulge your emotions, so don't hold back. Keep writing until you have broken through the layers of logic, then explore the feelings you find underneath.

This writing does not have to be shared with anyone unless you choose to share it. If you have difficulty expressing your feelings of love for your partner, try putting it in a note or card for your partner to read—no need to wait for a special occasion. You might be surprised at how pleased your partner will be!

The Second Born and the Only

These two birth orders tend to be drawn to each other immediately. The Second Born appreciates the Only's emotional expression and attention to detail, and the Second Born especially likes the advice the Only is wont to give freely. Advice is a suggestion on how to improve something, and the perfectionist streak in the Second Born loves that.

The Only likes the Second Born's dependability; such dependability lets the Only stick to the organized schedule that is so important in an Only's life. The Second Born's lack of emotional expression also appeals to an Only, because the Only can imagine how the Second Born must feel and doesn't have to relate to real feelings. And because the Second Born's peacemaking skills often translate into leaving other people alone, the Only can have as much privacy as he or she wants.

Of course, some of these traits, while complementing each other on the surface, can lead to serious misunderstandings.

Mike, a Second Born, and Jean, an Only, met shortly after high school and fell in love almost immediately. On their first date, they went out to eat. Mike asked Jean what she would like and ordered for her, and Jean entertained Mike with her animated story-telling. Mike loved the way Jean told stories; she related all the details, told the story in the order it happened and put the climax at the end where it belonged, all the while injecting drama and comedy with her expressions, gestures, voice, and eyes. Jean loved Mike's self-discipline and his ambition. He had done well in sports in high school, and he had done well in academics. He had a job during high school and earned enough to buy himself a car, which he kept in immaculate condition. They bonded throughout their courtship, doing a variety of activities when they dated, and eventually they married, a happy and united couple.

Then one day at dinner, Mike said the meal was good but mentioned that the peas were a little cold. Jean burst into tears and ran into the bedroom, leaving Mike sitting at the table, stunned.

Mike hadn't intended to hurt Jean's feelings. As a Second Born, it was natural for him to offer suggestions for improvement. He didn't mean anything unkind by it. After the cold peas episode, Mike, in Second Born peacemaking mode, began keeping his suggestions to himself, but his silence didn't help matters much. Jean still didn't feel good about the way Mike related to her.

It took some time for Mike to change his thought patterns so that he could think about how his wife felt. It was hard for him, because, as a Second Born, he preferred logic over emotion; he wasn't really aware of his own feelings, so it was difficult for him to think about hers. With effort, he eventually got better at relating to Jean emotionally, and he improved especially after he and Jean began leading a Sunday School class of young children—who taught Mike a lot about dealing with feelings.

Mike and Jean were able to work on their problems and make their relationship even stronger. The outcome for Ed and Elaine was not so fortunate.

In this case, Ed was the Only and Elaine was the Second Born. Like many Only/Second Born couples, they fell in love the first night they met, and they moved in together shortly afterwards. Unfortunately, when they moved in together, they stopped dating, and that inhibited the bonding that had begun on their first date.

Elaine loved Ed very much, and she expressed her love by trying to help him move toward perfection. When he combed his hair, she pointed out how it could be neater. When his shirt didn't quite match his pants, she suggested a different shirt. When he talked about his job, she told him how he could do his work better.

After a while, this "constructive criticism" began to wear on Ed, and his reactions became increasingly negative. Whenever Elaine made a suggestion, Ed balked, then got angry, and then put on a short but vivid display of violent emotion. "Can't you ever say anything good about what I do?" he'd demand. From his perspective as an Only, Ed began to view Elaine's suggestions as an intolerable intrusion.

Elaine didn't understand Ed's reactions; she felt he was being unreasonable. All she was trying to do was help him improve, which, to her, was a good and desirable thing, and he didn't appreciate her efforts. However, with the Second Born's sensitivity to negative emotions, Elaine, like Mike, stopped offering constructive criticism. She didn't give compliments; instead she just kept quiet. And when Ed offered her a compliment, she routinely deflected it, pointing out flaws that Ed hadn't mentioned. Not only did she make Ed feel as though he couldn't do anything well enough for her, by challenging his compliments, she made him feel as though she didn't value his opinion.

Unfortunately, Elaine and Ed were not able to change their own thinking to improve the way they related to each other, and eventually they parted company.

EXERCISE: When a Second Born offers correction or criticism, it is intended as a loving gesture to help the other person move toward perfection. To the Only Child, however, such correction feels like pressure; the Only Child wants to do things right and becomes anxious and frustrated when told he or she is doing something wrong.

Only and Second Born partners can remove the emotional sting from the Second Born's correction by treating it in a slightly more formal way. Onlies can invite the Second Born's opinion by asking, "Which do you think is better?" Second Borns can get permission to offer their opinions by asking, "May I make a suggestion?" This ritual turns Second Born correcting into a cooperative exercise—satisfying the Second Born's need to do better without making the Only feel as if he or she is under attack.

The Second Born and the First Born

When First Borns and Second Borns get together, the result can be a permanent relationship, but it often won't be a close one. Close relationships require an emotional connection, and neither First Borns nor Second Borns are very good at emotions. The First Born wants to know how others feel but has little awareness of his or her own feelings, while the Second Born keeps feelings locked firmly in the furthest recesses of his or her heart.

This same quality can attract these two birth orders. From the Second Born's point of view, a relationship with a First Born feels safe precisely because there is no emotional pressure. But the lack of emotional connection can exacerbate stress and unhappiness when problems show up in a marriage.

That's what happened to Jerry, a First Born, and Ann, a Second Born, who run a farm. When the farm economy began to flag, Jerry and Ann had financial problems, and they both got off-the-farm jobs to supplement their agricultural income. Jerry's parents also had a farm nearby, and they too had financial difficulties, so Jerry tried to help them as much as he could.

Ann, with her evaluative thinking, was able to see pitfalls as she continually assessed their situation. But when she offered her insights to Jerry, he felt guilty because he didn't think of these things himself. To avoid Ann's correction, he began to hide things from her, including major purchases. When Ann discovered these things, she felt hurt that he made these decisions without consulting her. And then, of course, Jerry felt doubly guilty—once for not thinking about the impact of his decisions, and again for bringing on Ann's corrections.

Jerry felt a great loyalty to his parents; he worked with them daily and felt they deserved his help because they raised him. Ann also had a great family loyalty, but hers was directed toward Jerry and their own children; she felt that Jerry put her and their children second behind his parents. Ann and Jerry didn't relate well enough to resolve this conflict. Jerry became defensive when Ann brought the subject up. He changed the subject or, failing that, tried to find fault with Ann—anything to avoid the tremendous sense of guilt that came upon him as a result of Ann's evaluation and correction.

Because of the difficulty Ann and Jerry have with their own feelings, neither is really able to understand the other. Their birth orders do not lend themselves to such understanding, and, in a situation fueled by outside stresses, the combination of First Born and Second Born doesn't lend itself to a harmonious relationship. Unless they are able to learn to connect with each other emotionally, Ann and Jerry are likely to end their marriage because of irreconcilable differences.

Not all First Born/Second Born relationships are doomed to failure. It just takes a little more work and self-awareness on each person's part to build an emotional connection that can withstand the trials and tribulations of marriage.

Dave, a Second Born, is in an unhappy marriage with his First Born wife, Abby, and is just beginning the sometimes painful process of self-examination. This is the second marriage for both of them; she has four children from her first marriage, and this is the chief source of problems for Dave and Abby.

Abby, as a First Born, demanded respect from the children by hollering at them. It didn't work, so Dave, sensitive to anger and seeking peace as a Second Born, tried coming to Abby's aid by doing what he knew how to do—imposing rules and punishing the children by taking away toys and privileges. Abby didn't like Dave's rule-making, so she turned her anger toward him.

His peacemaking efforts having failed, Dave suggested that Abby get a divorce. Dave didn't want a divorce; if he had wanted one, he would have filed for one. His suggestion was a ploy to try to get Abby to pay attention to his needs and take his feelings seriously. It didn't work, but he was able to get Abby to go to counseling with him.

In counseling, Dave can give a complete description—actually an evaluation—of his situation at home. He covers all the details, and he is confident of the conclusions he has drawn because he has looked at all the details. The one thing he can't share in counseling is an analysis of feelings in his household. As a Second Born, he keeps a tight lid on his own emotions so he won't have to deal with them, and he simply isn't aware of Abby's feelings or the feelings of her children. And because of this significant blind spot, he can't find a solution to the problems at home.

Dave is working on his ability to understand and cope with emotions, and he should be commended for his efforts, because dealing with emotions is so difficult for Second Borns. It will take some time and perseverance, but learning how to think about how Abby and her children feel will help Dave become better acquainted with his own feelings, and it will open up a whole range of new possibilities in meeting the challenges at home.

EXERCISE: First Borns and Second Borns can get in touch with their own feelings by writing down their thoughts and ideas. Writing can also help each comprehend how others feel, by writing from the other person's point of view. To do this, start with what you've learned about your partner's Birth Order Personality. For example, if your partner is a First Born, you could begin with what you know about how First Borns view the world—that there is no such thing as unconditional love, that good things are always just out of reach, and so on. If your partner is a Second Born, begin with the Second Born view of the world—that there is no love unless you're perfect, that nothing the Second Born does is really good enough, and so on. Then write about a specific incident, using your partner's words, gestures, and facial expressions to help you interpret that incident from your partner's point of view.

When you've finished, discuss your new insights with your partner. You don't have to let your partner read what you've written, but do tell what you believe he or she was thinking and feeling during that incident. Be open to the possibility that your interpretation isn't quite accurate, and ask your partner to correct you if you have misinterpreted something. This will feel awkward and a little uncomfortable at first, but as you become more accustomed to putting yourself in the other's place, your understanding of each other—and your ability to connect on an emotional level—will grow beyond anything you ever thought possible.

The Second Born and Other Second Borns

If we gave you the impression that First Borns and Second Borns have trouble establishing an emotional connection, it's nothing compared with the difficulty two Second Borns have with each other. Second Borns may think alike, share the same values and practice the same virtues of self-discipline, self-sacrifice, and logical thinking, but they don't express the emotion that typically draws two people together. They just aren't naturally drawn to each other.

The exception to this general rule is when substance abuse is involved. Using alcohol or drugs releases Second Borns from their emotional inhibitions, and they are able to make that connection that otherwise wouldn't be possible. Likewise, a shared traumatic event that allows them to see each other's emotional side might bring two Second Borns together.

Roger and Laurie met through their drug use. As they used together, they found an emotional connection, and that was strong enough to keep them dating. When they decided to marry, their self-discipline asserted itself, and they stopped using drugs.

Without the use of drugs to help them share their feelings, the way Roger and Laurie related to each other changed. It was no longer on an emotional basis, but on the basis of logic, rules, and self-discipline. They didn't argue except when they were being playful, and then they would argue for the fun of it, for the challenge of seeing who could win. Each became more of a perfectionist, encouraged, naturally, by the other. They divided the chores around the house, Laurie taking care of the interior and Roger being responsible for the yard and the outside of the house. Each had suggestions for the other, of course, and each readily accepted the other's input. Nothing was out of place; their home was beautiful inside and out.

Then came another huge change: They had children, two girls. As babies, the girls needed attention, affection, and positive interaction.

Laurie and Roger provided this in full measure—in fact, in rather too full measure.

With the Second Born's distaste for "unfair" compliments, Laurie and Roger praised everything their girls did, whether it was warranted or not. The results were dramatic and completely the opposite of what Laurie and Roger intended.

The older girl took the continual compliments to mean there were no boundaries for her, no rules, and no consequences. As a teenager, she and a friend took a bus halfway across the country, without bothering to tell anyone where they were going or what they were doing. You might think that this, finally, would be something Laurie and Roger could not bring themselves to praise, but they managed to find a way to compliment their daughter for her escapade. That simply led to more extreme behavior; after graduating from high school, the daughter moved on a whim to various parts of the country, got involved with drugs and generally lived with no sense of stability.

The effect of the constant compliments on the younger daughter was markedly different. To her, the compliments were something she had to reach for, trophies she had to win. But because she received compliments for everything she did, she began setting impossible goals for herself, and these impossible goals eventually sent her into a deep depression. She suffered a number of psychosomatic illnesses, could not work up the self-confidence she needed to make her life work the way she wanted it to, and felt utterly unable to have a strong, committed relationship herself. Her parents' constant praise defeated her even as it energized her sister.

There was no easy way for Roger and Laurie to avoid the consequences of their behavior with each other and their children. Without an understanding of their own and others' feelings, Roger and Laurie couldn't provide a rich and balanced emotional environment for themselves or their daughters.

EXERCISE: Many Second Borns have an all-or-nothing approach to criticism and praise. But continual compliments can be just as devastating to a relationship as continual correction. To find a happy medium—giving praise when it is due and offering constructive correction when it is warranted—Second Borns can start by separating the process from the end result of what their partners do. If your partner is considering returning to school so as to be eligible for a promotion at work, taking classes is the process; the promotion is the end result. Both of these might strike you as worthy, laudable things, and you would compliment your partner's foresight and willingness to work for what he or she wants. But if your partner is unhappy at his or her job, you might offer constructive correction about the end result. Going back to school—the process—still is deserving of compliments, but you might suggest another line of study that would allow your partner to get into a field he or she would enjoy more.

This approach to balancing praise and criticism will feel better to your partner because your compliments will carry conviction and your criticism will stem from your love for your partner.

The Second Born and the Third Born

When Second Borns and Third Borns get together, the Second Born typically is the female and the Third Born is the male— seldom the other way around. This may be because men in general tend to give higher priority to their careers and goals, while women tend to place a higher priority on relationships. In situations where this different orientation holds true, the Second Born man wouldn't find much to attract him to a Third Born woman. He is self-disciplined; she's a free spirit. He's logical in his thinking; she's geared more toward her emotions in her thinking. He's detail-oriented and aims for perfection; she finds details boring and aims for "good enough." Some Second Born men might find Third Born women refreshing, but, more often, Third Born women drive Second Born men crazy.

It's different when the birth orders are switched. Second Born women can see a lot of possibilities in relationships with Third Born men. The Third Born male's compassion, his desire to please, his attention to others' needs, and his heroic efforts to rescue others—literally or figuratively—all these traits appeal to the Second Born female.

The Third Born's natural instinct to rescue others, to make things better, can wreak havoc in combination with the Second Born's feelings of inadequacy. That's what happened to Len and Pat. Pat, a Second Born, grew up abused by her father and neglected by her mother. Len, a Third Born, was the super-rescuer who took Pat away from all the awful things that happened in her parents' house.

During the fifteen years of their marriage, Len was in rescuing mode continually. Every little mistake Pat made, every quirk of her complex personality was cause for him to rescue her. And every time Len jumped in to save her, Pat sank deeper and deeper into depression, because she felt woefully inadequate to cope with even the smallest things. This constant rescuing also raised a barrier between Len and Pat. Because of their roles as savior and victim, Len never approached Pat as a partner; he was always "above" her, and Pat never could connect with Len. The relationship continued to deteriorate until finally Len decided to leave. But even then, he was still trying to rescue Pat, checking in by phone with her every day, stopping by often and asking if there were anything he could do for her. Even after they divorced, even after Len remarried, he was still trying to rescue Pat.

Eventually, Pat put a stop to Len's calling and visiting. With the help of counseling, she was able to confront her emotions and deal with them instead of locking them away, and as her emotional health grew, so did her confidence in herself to handle her own life. She discovered she did not need to be rescued any longer.

EXERCISE: The Second Born's blind spot is thinking about how other people feel. The Third Born's blind spot is working with others as equals. By becoming more aware of body language and the feelings body language reveals, both Second Borns and Third Borns can diminish their blind spots: Second Borns can begin to recognize others' emotions and Third Borns can see others as individuals rather than victims.

Discuss the following body language expressions with your partner and help each other interpret what they mean.

- Crossed arms
- A frown
- Raised eyebrows
- A lively step
- High-pitched voice
- Low-pitched voice
- Finger-pointing
- Playing with the hair
- One leg wrapped around the other
- Kicking motion with the foot
- A single raised eyebrow
- A red face
- Squinting
- Hand at the side of the face
- Pulling on the earlobe
- Looking away while you're talking
- Looking at you while you're talking
- Answering you before you are done asking

If you think of other nonverbal messages, discuss them as well. You may find that your interpretations need a little refining, but you'll get better with practice.

The Second Born and the Fourth Born

On the surface, Second Borns and Fourth Borns seem to be compatible, especially in the way they think. The Second Born's tendency toward logic is designed to stifle emotions, while the Fourth Born's analytical mind looks for ways to control emotions. No wonder they get along, right?

Well, yes and no. The fact is, the Fourth Born, who grew up having to figure out all the older siblings just to survive, is a master at out-reasoning others—not because he or she is smarter, but because he or she has learned how to take control of a discussion or argument by changing its focus.

For example, let's say a Second Born woman mentions that the kitchen could use remodeling. It looks shabby, it's difficult to work in, and she has put up with it for a long time. This is how her Fourth Born husband might respond: "Do you think we're made of money? I work hard to make ends meet around here, and I don't want to blow our savings on just anything."

To the Second Born, this kind of response is the equivalent of a fast left hook; it comes out of nowhere and leaves her dazed and confused. The Fourth Born hasn't addressed any of the Second Born's points. Instead, he took the discussion about the need to redo the kitchen and turned it into a discussion about the household budget and how hard he works. The Second Born, who has spent her energy assembling the points in favor of a new kitchen, can't process what she perceives as a completely different topic, so she just gives up.

The Fourth Born also has learned to use anger as an effective tool to get what he or she wants. This works particularly well with the Second Born, who is highly sensitive to anger and desperately wants to keep the peace. The peacemaking Second Born, who tends to avoid confrontation if possible, is defenseless against the well-timed and finely gauged angry outburst of the Fourth Born.

If the Second Born discovers these patterns during courtship, he or she will tend to withdraw from the relationship. If the Second Born and the Fourth Born marry, they tend to stay together, even if the Second Born is unhappy, because the Second Born's self-discipline and adherence to rules will convince him or her to remain in the marriage.

That's not to say that Fourth Borns have it all their own way with Second Borns. Remember Andy, the Second Born man who kept changing jobs every time a promotion appeared on the horizon? Andy's wife was a Fourth Born who had learned how to adjust to life's difficulties without becoming victimized by them. She seldom complained, and she did her best to accommodate

Andy's somewhat erratic career path. Other birth orders might have lodged frequent strenuous complaints about Andy's lack of purpose and the financial strain it put on the family, but it took this accepting Fourth Born quite a long time to reach the end of her patience. When she finally had enough, she found a well-paying job herself and left Andy to continue his search for the "perfect" job on his own.

EXERCISE: The Second Born's natural reaction to anger is to try to find a way to make peace, but that can lead to more anger from a Fourth Born who needs people to stand up to him or her to feel mature. Sometimes, the most effective strategy for a Second Born confronted with a Fourth Born's angry outburst is to say, in a firm voice, "Stop it! It's like this…" Fourth Borns can counter the Second Born's passive peace-keeping by saying, "Tell me what's wrong with this." By inviting criticism, the focus is shifted from diffusing anger to making something better—a primary motivator for Second Borns.

Second Borns put pressure on themselves to be the best they can possibly be, believing that's the only way they become deserving of love. The Third Born's pressure comes from trying to be all things to all people all the time—a standard even Second Borns find too exacting. We put on our masks and capes in the next chapter to look at the world through the heroic eyes of the Third Born.

CHAPTER SIX

The Third Born

So you think superheroes only exist in cartoons and comic books? Truth is, they're all around us—police officers, firefighters, paramedics, social workers. And chances are these people are Third Borns. Maybe they can't leap tall buildings in a single bound, and they're not really faster than a speeding locomotive. But they are experts at rescuing people, and not just from danger. Third Borns will try to rescue people from poor decisions, from financial troubles, from unhappiness in general. Some of them get so focused on rescuing others that they ignore their own needs and, sometimes, their own best interests.

Third Borns rescue because they don't want other people to feel vulnerable, and they don't want others to feel vulnerable because they feel vulnerable themselves. Third Borns learned early on to hide their feelings of vulnerability under a cloak of emotional strength and are adept at showing the world that nothing bothers them.

Depending on their circumstances, Third Borns will fight their own vulnerability by becoming either fearful or fearless. The fearful type Third Born usually has a Second Born sibling of the opposite sex and will learn to avoid situations where he or she might feel afraid. The fearless type Third Born usually has a Second Born sibling of the same sex and will actively seek out frightening situations to prove that he or she is not afraid. The fearful Third Born will shy away from risk; the fearless Third Born will embrace risk. The result is the same for both types, however: Both end up being more afraid of fear than of anything else.

Third Borns have a hard time forming close relationships with others because being close means showing another person your soft underbelly—allowing yourself to be vulnerable. This is another reason why rescue work is so appealing to Third Borns. Those Third Borns in emergency services, such as police officers, firemen, and paramedics, can help others day and night while maintaining professional detachment. Such detachment is considered desirable and even necessary in these fields, so Third Borns get high marks for doing important work with the proper degree of emotional distance.

In personal relationships, the Third Born is able to preserve that distance by continually playing the role of rescuer. Rescuers are strong and capable; victims are weak and helpless. As long as the Third Born is rescuing someone, he or she doesn't have to relate to that person as an individual.

One Third Born man demonstrated his detachment on his first date with the woman he eventually married. He was a police officer, so for their first date he invited the woman to ride along with him on patrol. The trappings of his job—the uniform, the badge, the lights and siren, the radio—all established an atmosphere of authority and protection radiating from this Third Born man, disguising any vulnerability he felt. The woman was willing on this first date to relate to him in terms of his job, and he felt safe enough with her response to ask her out again. As they continued dating, he was able to open up gradually to her and finally, after they had been dating about three months, he announced to her: "I don't need to be a cop all the time now."

EXERCISE: Imagine you are two years old, building an intricate edifice with blocks. Your older sister knocks the blocks down when you aren't looking, but you know she did it. You go crying to Mom, who, having heard the same complaint countless times, sighs and tells you to ignore your sister. You try this new tactic and are amazed at the results. No matter what your sister does—teasing, messing around with your toys, making faces at you—you ignore her. Unable to get a reaction out of you, your sister eventually gives up and leaves you alone. It works! You have found the secret to protect yourself from others and from now on you won't let anything bother you.

When you can feel taunts and teasing sliding off an invisible shell around you, you are experiencing what it feels like to be a Third Born.

There's Nothing to Do!

Third Borns hate being bored almost as much as they hate feeling vulnerable. They're perfectly happy to sit down to a nice dinner and have a lively conversation with family and friends, but once the meal is over, they'll be looking around for something else to do. Third Borns don't linger over their after-dinner coffee and they'll grow restless if their companions dally too long. They want to get up and move on to the next thing.

This is where the Third Born's spontaneity comes from. If something looks or sounds interesting to them, they're off like a shot to investigate—especially if they're engaged in something that doesn't particularly interest them. Third Borns, unlike Onlies, welcome interruptions because they ward off boredom, and they love it when friends or relatives stop by unannounced. Routine, so comforting to other birth order personalities, can frustrate the Third Born if it goes on without variation for too long.

Though many Third Borns aren't even aware of it, what they call boredom is really loneliness. Third Borns usually are friendly to just about everybody and will have dozens of acquaintances, but they protect themselves from being vulnerable by keeping most people at arm's length. Typically, a Third Born will have only one or two bosom buddies with whom he or she can share feelings. When those connections aren't available, the Third Born feels lonely. But because loneliness implies vulnerability, the Third Born renames the feeling as boredom.

EXERCISE: Third Borns need variety in their daily lives to combat boredom. When a Third Born says there's nothing to do, what he or she really means is that it's time for something different; but often it's difficult to think of new and different things to do. If this happens often in your house, consider making a list of possible activities and keeping it on the refrigerator or next to your calendar. These activities can be projects around the house; a list of restaurants you want to try sometime; movies, plays or concerts you want to see; or other recreational activities like camping, fishing, and so on. Many local newspapers publish a weekly or monthly calendar of events, as well; pull these sections out and mark the things that interest you. Then, when you or your partner feels boredom creeping in, you'll have a menu of options ready and waiting.

Keeping Up with the Joneses

Third Borns think by comparing. On the job, they'll weigh the type and amount of work they do against the type and amount their coworkers do. Around the neighborhood, they compare the sizes of the houses, the landscaping, even the vehicles in the driveway. At the grocery store, they consider the size of a package and the price and make their purchase decision after careful comparison of all the choices.

This style of thinking makes the Third Born more interested in the bottom line than in the details. He or she wants a simple conclusion that lends itself to comparison—this is good, that's bad, this is fun, that's boring, etc. Comparison lets the Third Born decide whether he or she is making progress, whether things are the way he or she hoped they would be, and whether he or she needs to make any changes.

In some cases, this comparison thinking can lead the Third Born to question his or her relationships, career, even lifestyle. This isn't necessarily negative. The Third Born cop we told you about earlier often asks his wife why she thinks they get along so well compared with other couples they know. He compares the way other couples argue, the way they joke together, even the way they manage their finances. This comparison reassures him that his relationship is as solid as he thinks it is and thus reduces his sense of vulnerability.

EXERCISE: Comparison thinking can be destructive when it takes the focus off what you want and puts it on what everyone else wants or seems to have. When this happens, you can find yourself chasing an elusive American dream without appreciating or valuing what is already present in your life. This exercise will help you make sure the goals and dreams you are pursuing are your own—and make you more aware of what you already have.

Make two columns on a sheet of paper. Title the first column "What I Have Now." Under this heading, list the things you have in your life right now in every category—relationship, family, career, home, auto, finances, recreation. Include everything you can think of on this list; don't be surprised if you need more than one sheet to complete it.

Now, title the second column "Things I Want." These are the things you'd like to have in each of the categories from the first list. For example, if you live in an apartment in the city, but someday you'd like to buy an acreage in the country, that will go under the "Things I Want" heading, even if "someday" is far in the future. Leave a space under each item on this list. In that space, write the reason you want this item. You might want that house in the country so your children will have a big yard to play in, or so you can raise chickens. Be honest about your reasons. If you want a new car because your best friend just got a new car, that's OK, but it's important to acknowledge that this is the real reason you want a new car.

After you've completed your lists, put them away somewhere for one week and resolve not to do anything about any item in the "Things I Want" column for that week. At the end of the week, read your lists over again. You may find that some of the items in your "Things I Want" column don't apply, or the reasons for them have changed. You may even have some items to add under "What I Have Now." This is good. It means you are focused on appreciating what you have and listening to your own feelings about what you want.

Lean on Me

Deep down, Third Borns believe they cannot be loved if they're not strong. When they were kids, older brothers and sisters picked on them if they betrayed any sign of vulnerability. Mom and Dad may have told the Third Born to ignore the siblings' taunts and expressed approval when the Third Born followed their advice. This sent two strong messages to the Third Born: People won't try to hurt you if they think you're strong, and others will be pleased if you act strong.

By the time they reach adulthood, Third Borns are so good at appearing to be strong that often they don't know how not to be strong. They believe that if they aren't strong, they'll disappoint someone, and they sure don't want to do that. So they go on being strong day after day, giving their energy, their support, sometimes even their money to others, who may or may not appreciate it.

Becca, a Third Born woman in her twenties, was so enmeshed in helping others and being strong for others that it took her years to realize her live-in boyfriend was taking advantage of her. As a Third Born, she wanted to please him, and she prided herself on her ability to let things roll off her back—a manifestation of the typical Third Born "it doesn't bother me" attitude. The more demands her boyfriend placed on her, the more Becca would tell herself that she had to be strong for him. To get her to do what he wanted, all he had to do was act like he needed her help. Even after Becca realized what her boyfriend was doing, it took her quite a long time to decide to leave the relationship because she still wanted to please him. And for nearly a year after she left, she still found herself taking her ex-boyfriend's calls any time he said he needed something from her.

EXERCISE: When Third Borns are in rescuing mode, they don't look at others' strengths; they see only the weaknesses. To break out of this habit, write down your partner's strengths in the following areas. If you have trouble coming up with strengths, think about the things you admire in your partner and list them in the appropriate category.

- Emotional strengths
- Mental strengths
- Physical strengths
- Spiritual strengths
- Social strengths
- Other strengths

When you've finished your list, share it with your partner. He or she might be surprised at what you've come up with.

Back Off!

Third Borns don't really have a defense system to help them cope with their feelings of vulnerability. They have learned not to let those feelings show, and they keep most people around them at a safe emotional distance so they won't have to acknowledge their vulnerability. But feelings don't go away just because you cover them up, and just covering them up doesn't provide a defense. So when Third Borns reach the end of their ability to cover up their feelings—and for many Third Borns it takes a lot to reach this point—they are apt to go on the attack. It's like a pendulum swinging. At one extreme, Third Borns are agreeable, aiming to please, happy to help anyone with anything. At the other extreme, Third Borns get angry and, lacking any other defense, begin attacking others.

When a Third Born has reached this point, you might hear him or her say something like, "That's it, I'm done," or, "Everybody wants a piece of me and I'm tired of it, so I'm not going to do it anymore." When a Third Born has had enough, it's usually because he or she feels used or taken advantage of. And that feeling is related to the Third Born's conviction that he or she cannot be loved unless he or she is strong.

Imagine how tiring it must be to be strong all the time. Nobody can do that, not even the most determined Third Born. There are times when, even if it's just out of sheer emotional exhaustion, Third Borns cannot be strong. If they're not strong, they're vulnerable, and if they're vulnerable, they feel cornered. So, if they can't cover up their vulnerability with strength, they go on the offensive. They may become critical of others ("Why can't you take care of yourself?") or they may complain about their responsibilities ("I have to do everything around here!") or they may, obliquely, acknowledge their feelings of not being lovable ("When do I get to do something for me?").

At these times, Third Borns may want others to leave them alone; they may even demand it. Reassurance that they are loved for who they are, weaknesses and all, can help assuage their feelings of vulnerability and, with practice, can even allow them to become comfortable with saying, "No."

EXERCISE: Third Borns tend to do for others rather than for themselves, sometimes draining their own resources so much that they become desperate to do something for themselves. To keep the pendulum's arc from going to extremes, make a list of things you have done for yourself and things you can do for yourself. Ask your partner for suggestions for the list, and remember that little things are just as important as big things—a bubble bath, a walk in the park, a favorite TV show or a favorite meal are all small things you can do for yourself that will make a big difference in how you feel about doing for others. When you look over your list, you might discover that you do more for yourself than you realize. But if you're a typical Third Born, you'll probably be shocked to find how little you do for yourself. This awareness, plus the suggestions for things you can do for yourself, will help you bring the pendulum to a more reasonable swing.

The Third Born and the Only

This is a fairly common combination in marriage, possibly because Third Borns and Onlies both are able to express their emotions. In fact, their nonverbal emotional communication is so similar that it's easy to confuse these two birth order personalities.

Still, there are areas where Third Borns and Onlies can run into conflict. For example, the Third Born expresses love by helping, and this can make the Only feel smothered. The Only needs time alone, but the Third Born usually wants to be alone only when he or she is feeling unhappy, so the Third Born can misinterpret the Only's desire for time apart. The Only's schedules and organization can make the Third Born feel bored or trapped or both, while the Third Born's ability to change directions or plans in a flash can be highly stressful for the Only.

When there is conflict, Third Borns and Onlies usually are able to find ways to accommodate each other, even if they don't fully understand each other. The Third Born wants to please his or her partner and will give the Only time alone if it makes the Only happy. The Only can tolerate the Third Born's spontaneity as long as the Only can think of plans as tentative rather than firm. These two birth order personalities will go to great lengths to give each other what they think the other wants.

Tom and Kate are a good example of this kind of accommodation. Kate is the Only and Tom is a fearful type Third Born. They fell in love and decided to live together, and they planned to get married. They chose a date and made all the arrangements, but a few days before the wedding Tom backed out. Of course, Kate was devastated, but after their chosen wedding date passed, they got back together and began talking about a new wedding date.

Tom didn't back out because he and Kate were having problems. He backed out because he was overcome with fear. After the first wedding date passed, his fear subsided, he started feeling better about his relationship with Kate, and he was ready to try planning their wedding again.

As an Only, Kate thinks with her feelings, so she could understand Tom's reaction to his own feelings. She could even accept what would be hard for other birth order personalities to believe—that Tom's reluctance to get married was based only on his own fear and not in any reservations he had about her. To other birth orders, Tom's actions would have felt like disrespect, unreliability, disloyalty or rejection. But Kate was able to understand Tom's point of view and was able to reorganize herself around the new wedding plans.

EXERCISE: The Third Born's spontaneity can clash with the Only's organization, but frustration over these two styles can be reduced significantly when the Third Born decides to do some things according to a plan. This takes some special thought on the Third Born's part, especially for the fearless type Third Born, but here are some things you can do:

◆ If you're in the mood to go out to eat, suggest doing it tomorrow instead of today.

◆ Suggest inviting company over next weekend instead of this weekend.

◆ Suggest going for a ride after dinner instead of right now.

◆ Instead of planning a surprise party for your Only partner, suggest having a party, then plan it with your partner.

By giving your partner some time to prepare for activities you want to do, you reduce the potential for stress in your Only partner. And because organization and knowing what is ahead is important to your partner, remember to talk to your partner about any plans before you suggest those plans to someone else.

The Third Born and the First Born

Third Borns usually are attracted to First Borns who make them feel safe. This First Born doesn't place demands on the Third Born; instead, he or she listens to the Third Born, agrees with the Third Born and values the Third Born's ideas and opinions. When the Third Born talks, the First Born looks at the Third Born, nods in agreement and asks questions to indicate that he or she has been listening. This type of First Born is no threat to the Third Born, so the Third Born can relax.

Fearful type Third Borns often find First Borns more appealing than fearless type Third Borns do because of this feeling of safety. These Third

Borns feel comfortable in the relationship and very rarely look to leave. In fact, others may be puzzled by this Third Born's willingness to accept behavior that they never would tolerate.

Brenda was one such Third Born. Her First Born husband, Joe, was unfaithful to her, and Brenda's friends urged her to leave him. They thought she should be offended at Joe's behavior. But she was ready to forgive him, and she continually looked for ways to restore the relationship. When he moved out, she kept contacting him, pleading with him and making promises she thought would please him. She even offered to give him time to figure out what he wanted rather than pressuring him to come home. She was partially successful in that he did return home for a time, but eventually he ended the marriage.

Peter, a fearless type Third Born, didn't have the same kind of accommodating attitude with Jessica, his First Born wife. He was drawn to her out of a sense of sympathy for the bad experiences she had endured, and he married her to give her a better life. He also took on the job of making her a better person. He told her how to act, how to dress, how to behave with others, how to deal with the children; in virtually every area of her life, he had advice on how she should proceed. From a Second Born, this kind of advice would be a reflection of the Second Born's drive for perfection. But from a Third Born, this is another way of rescuing someone. The message is, "You don't know how to do this, so I'll help you."

Peter felt put off when he sensed that Jessica wasn't exactly thrilled with his efforts to improve her. But their relationship got better when he began to view her as a competent person, and she began to trust her own capabilities. Peter still gives Jessica ideas from time to time on what she should do and how she should do it, but Jessica doesn't feel compelled to follow his suggestions, and Peter doesn't feel rejected if she decides to do things her own way.

EXERCISE: Third Borns who are in rescuing mode tend to believe that others need their help, and they seldom distinguish between times when help truly is needed and times when it would be appreciated. When your

Third Born partner asks, "Do you need help?" you can clarify the difference by saying, "No, I don't need help, but I would appreciate you giving me a hand." This phrasing breaks the Third Born's concentration on rescuing and puts you and your partner on a more equal footing to get the job done.

If you're a Third Born worried about playing the rescuer too often, train yourself to ask, "Would you like some help?" instead of saying, "Do you need help?" Ask your partner to correct you when you slip into your rescuing role by using the phrasing above.

The Third Born and the Second Born

Third Borns and Second Borns can have wonderful relationships. The Second Born likes the Third Born's freedom of emotional expression, and the Second Born's dependability helps the Third Born feel safe. Their senses of humor are similar, too, although the Second Born's mock-serious teasing can confuse and wound the Third Born.

Deborah, a fearful type Third Born, had this difficulty with her Second Born husband, Ben. They had been married for more than forty years; Deborah had been unhappy for most of the marriage and finally decided she had to get some help. Ben was content in the relationship, and he didn't mistreat her, but she felt that she might have to give up on the marriage because she was so miserable.

The problem turned out to be relatively simple: She didn't recognize his teasing as humor. She took Ben's teasing seriously and felt that he did it on purpose to make her feel bad. When she was told that this was Ben's sense of humor, she had a hard time believing it at first, but when she was able to accept that premise, she began to feel better.

As she examined more of Ben's behavior, Deborah realized that there, too, she had misread his sense of humor. She had felt that Ben was always trying to control her. Whenever she wanted to buy something or do something, or even when she had an idea, Ben would say something negative. When she recognized that he was teasing even in these situations, she was able to respond with her own sense of humor, and she felt more comfortable in the relationship.

Deborah had stayed in her relationship much longer than other people would have if they had been as unhappy as she was. She stayed because she was a fearful Third Born, unwilling to take the risk of being alone; it was safer to stay with her husband, even when she thought he was being mean to her.

The Third Born's desire to please and the Second Born's penchant for correction also can cause problems in a relationship. This was the issue for Marty, a Third Born, and Sarah, a Second Born.

Marty felt discouraged because he felt he couldn't please Sarah. He would mow the lawn, and Sarah would point out that it would have looked nicer if he had done it diagonally. He would cook dinner and have it ready for her when she got home from work, and she would say that baked potatoes would have been better than mashed tonight. As a Third Born, Marty wanted to please Sarah; as a Second Born, Sarah looked for ways to improve things instead of expressing pleasure at Marty's efforts.

Understanding birth order helped Marty and Sarah learn to appreciate each other. Marty discovered that he could find satisfaction in doing something for Sarah rather than in her reaction to what he did. Sarah came to understand her own desire for perfection and, just as important, that Marty did not share this drive. She was able to appreciate the things he did without worrying about how to improve them; instead, she focused her perfectionist tendencies on the things she did herself. Now that they know about birth order, Marty and Sarah are able to chuckle at each other's foibles instead of becoming irritated by them.

EXERCISE: Second Borns like details—the more, the better—but Third Borns tend to gloss over the details to get to the bottom line. You can practice giving your Second Born partner the details he or she craves by saying, "I've been thinking…" When you begin with this phrase, even if you don't spill all the details right away, your Second Born will ask questions that will elicit the details.

Using this technique also gives the Third Born an opportunity to use his or her considerable powers of persuasion. For example, you could ask your partner, "Do you want to go away for the weekend?" But this is likely to generate a simple yes or no, or a series of objections. But suppose you say, "I've been thinking. It's been six weeks since you and I have had a weekend away. There's a special discount on hotel rooms this weekend, plus we could go to that concert we talked about, and we could even stop by that little antique shop and see if they still have that lamp we liked." Here you've given your Second Born details, and if he or she wants more, he or she will say, "Can we get someone to feed the dog on such short notice?"

The Third Born and Other Third Borns

The Third/Third marriage can be the most compatible relationship out there. The usual Third Born pairing is a fearless male with a fearful female; in this relationship, she needs protecting and he is able to provide it. Third Borns are drawn together and often held together by their sense of humor. Even in trying times, they can joke with each other, and they understand each other because their sense of humor is the same.

When two Third Borns seek counseling, it's usually because the fearless one is taking risks that make the fearful one feel insecure. The fearful Third Born wants others to play it safe and knows that the risks the fearless Third Born is willing to take can be threatening. If the fearless Third Born is able to curb the risk-taking, these two can get along very well.

Two Third Borns rarely seem to break up, but it can happen. Lou and Sandy, both fearless Third Borns, became extremely aggressive toward each other, attacking each other any way they could. Their divorce was rancorous and unpleasant, and they felt ill will toward each other long after the split.

EXERCISE: Typically, two Third Borns will joke continually with each other. That can make it hard to connect, because humor tends to establish distance and close a subject. But you can use humor as a bridge instead of a door.

When your partner cracks a joke, respond with humor of your own, then continue with the same subject. For instance, if you suggest going out on the town, your partner might kid about going to a strip club for "real excitement." You can respond to that in a way that recognizes the humor—"You'd like that, wouldn't you?"—and follow with, "I was thinking we could go see the play at the community theater."

The Third Born and the Fourth Born

Third Borns and Fourth Borns seem to have a pretty balanced relationship for the most part, especially if the Fourth Born doesn't carry a lot of anger. The Third Born's efforts to please can help the Fourth Born feel wanted, and the Fourth Born's child-like qualities can make the Third Born feel strong and protective. The Third Born is sympathetic and the Fourth Born is empathetic, and the Third Born's put-down sense of humor is similar to the insulting quality of the Fourth Born's humor.

Sometimes, Third Born and Fourth Born qualities can clash, though. Third Borns want others to be happy and will do whatever they can to make that happen. When Fourth Borns react angrily to the Third Born's efforts, the Third Born feels unappreciated and unloved. On the other hand, Fourth Borns can bring on the Third Born's rescuing attempts by talking about how hard things are. This is one of the Fourth Born's ways of affirming his or her maturity, but to the Third Born, it's a cry for help.

When Eileen, a Third Born, tried to make things easier for Walter, his Fourth Born feelings of immaturity were aroused and he became angry. To him, Eileen's efforts to help implied that he was too immature to do things on his own; he needed the challenge of doing things himself to feel grown-up. Once Eileen understood this and stopped trying to rescue Walter, their relationship improved.

EXERCISE: Humor can be a difficult area for Third Borns and Fourth Borns because the Third Born's put-down sense of humor often is self-directed, while the Fourth Born's insulting humor is directed at others. Third Borns sometimes have trouble thinking of the insults as funny, but if you respond to your Fourth Born's insults with self-directed put-downs, both of you will be better able to understand and enjoy each other's humor.

Here are some examples of Fourth Born insults and possible Third Born responses:

◆ Fourth Born: "That was stupid."
   Third Born: "Yeah, I sure am stupid. I'm so stupid I don't even know how stupid I am—it's a good thing I have you around to tell me!"
◆ Fourth Born: "You can't do anything for yourself!"
   Third Born: "Boy, am I glad you're here to remind me how helpless I am. Otherwise I might get to thinking that I can do all kinds of things. Be sure to let me know when I can't do something."
◆ Fourth Born: "You're just using me."
   Third Born: "That's right! I'm so useless that I have to use you, or I would get nowhere. I'm sure glad you're here so I can use you!"

To other birth orders, these exchanges may appear rude and unkind. But this kind of repartee allows both Third Borns and Fourth Borns to find what's funny in each other's particular brand of humor. In many ways—not just humor—Fourth Borns are the hardest people to understand, because their view of the world is so different from the other birth orders. We analyze the fascinating Fourth Born next.

CHAPTER SEVEN

The Fourth Born

The world can feel like a cold and lonely place for the Fourth Born. No one—except other Fourth Borns—really understands how the Fourth Born thinks and feels. No one else had to grow up with quite the same set of challenges the Fourth Born faced, and, because the Fourth Born usually is the youngest, none of the other birth orders had to devote any energy to figuring out the Fourth Born. The other birth orders were older, bigger, and stronger, and that's all they needed to keep the Fourth Born in line.

But the Fourth Born had to figure out all of the personalities in his or her life simply to get through the day. The better the Fourth Born understood the siblings, the better the Fourth Born could avoid getting pushed around. This reality makes the Fourth Born a master at analyzing others' behaviors, emotions, and motives and, if the Fourth Born chooses, at manipulating others.

This pattern of analysis may help explain why Fourth Borns tend to be suspicious of others. One Fourth Born man found that it became very difficult for him to be nice to other people because, as he put it, "Whether I was nice to someone else or someone else was nice to me, it was going to end up costing me. So why bother?" He had learned that oftentimes others were nice to him because they wanted something in return; even when that wasn't the case, he believed his suspicions eventually would be proven valid. And when he did something nice for someone else, he found his own motives being questioned or, just as bad, he began to feel that others expected him to be nice.

In fact, being a nice guy made this man feel trapped. If someone did something nice for him, he knew that at some point he'd be expected to return the favor; he felt trapped in that cycle before it even began. Likewise, if he did something nice for someone once, he was convinced that he would be trapped into being nice to that person all the time, whether he felt like it or not. This feeling of being trapped is common among Fourth Borns and may be a reflection of the sense of helplessness they experienced as children, at the mercy of older siblings.

Much of the Fourth Born's view of the world is colored by painful childhood experiences. As children, Fourth Borns were continually told they were too young, too small, too weak or too immature to participate in activities with older siblings. Often, these messages persist into adulthood, and even grown-up Fourth Borns can have a hard time believing in their own maturity.

Worse, Fourth Born adults often have difficulty believing that others want them around. After all, no one wanted them around when they were kids—that's what all those "too young, too weak, etc." messages really meant—and Fourth Borns got used to the idea that they weren't supposed to tag along unless they were specifically invited. As adults, Fourth Borns still feel unwanted; they tend to be uncomfortable in large groups and may withdraw, even if the group is family. They tend to decline blanket invitations, believing that such invitations don't apply to them unless they are asked specifically to join the group.

One woman in her fifties still feels that others ignore her. She describes what she commonly experiences in large groups, such as staff meetings at her workplace: "If I interject something into the conversation, people will go on talking just as if I never said anything. It gives me the most awful feeling of being non-existent."

In the *Home Alone* movies, Kevin McAllister is the youngest child in a large family. His older brothers and sisters regard him as a pest; they never save any cheese pizza for him; they bar him from their rooms and tell him to get lost when they're with their friends; and, if all else fails, they ignore him in hopes that he'll just go away. This pattern is so deeply imbedded in the family's behavior that when they leave for a Christmas vacation, no one notices that Kevin has been left behind.

For Fourth Borns, this scenario isn't just the premise for a popular Hollywood comedy. This is their life, and there's nothing funny about it.

EXERCISE: Imagine you are four years old. You want to play with your older siblings, but they keep running off, leaving you alone. They keep telling you that you're not big enough to play with them. One day, they ask you to get the ball for them. You eagerly run after the ball, thinking that you'll be allowed to play with them after doing this favor. But when you get back with the ball, they again tell you to go away; you're still not big enough to play with them. Now you are alone, feeling used and angry, and resolving never to get taken like that again.

When you can feel the hurt of rejection and growing suspicion of others' motives, you are experiencing what it's like to be a Fourth Born.

"Life Is Hard"

Do you have a friend or coworker who uses this phrase a lot? That person might be a Fourth Born; the idea that "life is hard" has been pounded into Fourth Borns from their earliest days. In general, Fourth Borns experience the most injustice from their siblings—and sometimes even from their parents—which makes Fourth Borns feel that getting justice is hard. Indeed, many Fourth Borns feel there really is no justice in the world, and all they can do is try to get even when they've been wronged. As children, Fourth Borns were virtually powerless against older siblings, who could take away toys, attention, the TV remote or the best seat on the couch at will, which teaches the Fourth Born to work especially hard to keep control of possessions. And those older siblings always were doing things that were difficult for the Fourth Born to do—they could run faster, read better, play more complicated games—which leads the Fourth Born to think that, if he just tries hard enough, he'll be included in the older kids' activities. Fourth Borns have to work so hard as children to catch up to their older siblings that it becomes not only a lifelong habit, but a virtually unshakable view of how the world works.

From the Fourth Born point of view, working hard is the equivalent of growing up. All those things that the older kids can do are hard for the younger Fourth Born, so the Fourth Born assumes that those things are hard for the older kids, too. And if the older kids are working hard, then that's what the Fourth Born needs to do to feel grown-up.

This philosophy makes it very difficult for the Fourth Born to relax. It's not uncommon for adult Fourth Borns to be continually on the move at work and at home. A Fourth Born woman may sit down to watch TV, but she'll fold the laundry while she's watching. A Fourth Born man may attend the family reunion, but chances are he'll spend most of his time tending to the hot dogs and hamburgers on the grill. To these Fourth Borns, there is no distinction between relaxation and laziness. If a particular task is easy, it isn't really worthwhile, and if you should compliment a Fourth Born on doing an easy task, he or she is likely to feel that you're being condescending.

Want to really surprise and please a Fourth Born? Tell the Fourth Born woman folding the laundry in front of the television, "You really work hard around the house, don't you? I can tell it means a lot to you." Just the acknowledgment of the hard work they put in is very gratifying to Fourth Borns; the hard work makes them feel mature, but the compliment makes them feel noticed.

Fourth Borns who really feel that hard work equals maturity often decide not to offer their help to someone else faced with a difficult task. Fourth Borns don't want others to feel immature, so they'll let the other person do the hard work on their own. Helping, in the Fourth Born's view, would imply that the other person is too immature to finish the job.

EXERCISE: Fourth Borns sometimes have a tough time relaxing because they believe they can be loved only if they work hard all the time. You can encourage your Fourth Born partner to relax—and acknowledge his or her feelings of maturity—by making "play time" a reward for the hard work he or she has put in. By saying, "You've worked hard this week, and you've earned dinner at a nice restaurant," you let the Fourth Born know that you've noticed his or her efforts and you make him or her feel wanted by offering a night out. This kind of phrasing also circumvents the Fourth Born's natural suspicions because you've put the reason for the reward right out front.

What's That Supposed to Mean?

The Fourth Born is always analyzing, always wondering "what if," always trying to figure out what other people are thinking and feeling. Because of this, the Fourth Born seldom takes the words or actions of other people at face value; that would be too easy. As you can imagine, this can make genuine communication with Fourth Borns difficult, because they often attribute motives and emotions to others that exist only in their analysis.

An integral part of this analytical thinking pattern is the Fourth Born's inherent distrust of other people. Fourth Borns are always on the lookout for traps set for them by other people. Even a simple "hello" can appear threatening to a Fourth Born. They are so accustomed to being ignored that they suspect ulterior motives virtually everywhere. It may be that the person who says "hello" to a Fourth Born is just being civil. But it might be that this person wants something from the Fourth Born and is trying to disarm him with a pretense of friendliness. The Fourth Born may respond, albeit warily, or he may pass on his way without acknowledging the greeting.

When this distrust is especially pronounced, Fourth Borns will often try to get others to justify their behavior and "prove" their sincerity. One counselor in a prison ran into this from a Fourth Born inmate, who told her, "You're just here for the money. You don't care about us." If the counselor had risen to the bait, she would have found herself pushed into a cycle of continually proving that she cared. Instead, she told the inmate, "You can think that if you want." The inmate walked away and didn't try to challenge her motives again.

EXERCISE: Fourth Borns often don't believe much of anything they hear from other people—especially any sentiment that indicates others like them, appreciate them or want them around. But you can overcome that disbelief by confronting it at the outset. For instance, if you say, "I really enjoy talking with you," the Fourth Born won't believe you're sincere. On the other hand, if you say, "This might be hard to believe, but I really enjoy our conversations," the Fourth Born's trust in your sincerity jumps exponentially. Acknowledging the Fourth Born's tendency to distrust allows the Fourth Born to step back from that rote behavior and make a conscious decision to believe or disbelieve the expressed sentiment.

It's Not My Fault

Fourth Born children—especially those who are the youngest in their families—make convenient scapegoats for older siblings. If there were a way to pin something on the Fourth Born, the older kids would often do it, and the Fourth Born would be on the defensive regardless of his or her actual responsibility for the infraction. This makes blame of any kind a source of anger for Fourth Borns. In the extreme, even a request for information ("Did you pay the phone bill?" for instance) can trigger an angry outburst from a Fourth Born if he or she thinks you're trying to assign blame.

To others, this defensiveness can look like the Fourth Born's attempt to avoid taking responsibility for his or her own actions. It's the "devil made me do it" defense that seldom makes sense to other birth order personalities. But it makes perfect sense from the Fourth Born point of view.

If they are scapegoats for their older siblings in childhood, and especially if they are punished for things they didn't do, Fourth Borns grow up believing that there is no such thing as justice. They learn that they can't expect others to treat them fairly. So, if there is no justice from other people, the only option Fourth Borns have is to fight back and get even. By this rationale, Fourth Borns' actions are, to themselves, justified by the actions of others.

This pattern is particularly prevalent among Fourth Borns who carry a lot of anger. Usually, these angry Fourth Borns experienced a lot of injustice as children, so their eye-for-an-eye philosophy is especially pronounced. As adults, they believe that their behavior is governed by the behavior of those around them, and it seems perfectly logical to them: If you hadn't done this, I wouldn't have done that. Therefore, it's your fault I did that; I had no choice.

In our court system, we call this the "blame the victim" attitude. People charged with violent crimes—assault, rape, murder—will attempt to justify their actions by arguing that the victim brought on the abuse by his or her behavior. The assault victim said something snotty to the attacker; the rape victim wore suggestive clothing; the murder victim bullied and belittled the killer. This same pattern holds true in domestic abuse (the idea that the abused partner brought on the beating by his or her actions) and even in child sexual abuse, when the abuser attempts to shift responsibility onto the victim.

It is an unfortunate fact that angry Fourth Borns seem to be over-represented in our prison populations. It also is a fact that not all Fourth Borns are burdened by anger, and even those who do carry such a burden can learn to give it up through professional counseling.

EXERCISE: Anyone can carry anger around, but it's especially common among Fourth Borns because, of all the birth order person-alities, they tend to experience the most injustice. This exercise is beneficial for anyone who has experienced injustice—in other words, all of us.

You and your partner take turns being "It." When it's your turn, recall the most recent injustices you have experienced, but—this is very important—do NOT tell your partner. Simply nod your head when you recall an injustice; at this signal, your partner will say, "It's OK for you to forgive that person." Nod your head each time such a memory has come to mind. Each time you nod, your partner will repeat the same phrase: "It's OK for you to forgive that person."

We don't want you to share your memories in this exercise because sharing may tempt you or your partner to sympathize with each other rather than giving each other permission to forgive. Sympathy allows us to relive our injustices, but it doesn't release anger. We let go of anger only when we forgive.

The wording is important, too. Be sure that you and your partner say, "It's OK for you to forgive that person." Subconsciously, any other phrasing will only let you decide to forgive, which is not the same as actually forgiving.

If you find yourself overwhelmed by a memory, take a break. Pay attention to your feelings. When they have subsided, go back to the exercise, starting with this memory.

You may be surprised at how many instances of injustice you will recall from every stage of your life, from early childhood to last week. It isn't uncommon to go through forty or fifty such memories at a time. In fact, for a few days after doing this exercise, you may find yourself remembering more instances. When that happens, say to your partner, "I've got another one," and your partner will respond with, "It's OK to forgive that person."

You might feel like talking about some of your memories later. Wait until you have slept on this impulse before sharing any of your memories with your partner. This will allow your subconscious to process both the memory and the permission to forgive.

You Belong to Me

This can be a beautiful sentiment in a poem or a song, but in real life it causes much unhappiness and sometimes even violence. Fourth Borns who feel this way about their partners don't look at them as individuals but as possessions. And they can go to extremes to keep their possessions.

Again, this behavior was learned in childhood. Older siblings took toys away from the Fourth Born. The toy may have belonged to the older child in the first place, but the Fourth Born didn't understand that, especially when very young. All the Fourth Born knew was that he couldn't seem to keep a single thing he wanted, and that felt awful. Such Fourth Borns may decide at a young age that they will never allow anyone to take things away from them when they grow up.

These Fourth Borns can become pack rats. They keep everything, even if they don't want, need or use it anymore, just because not keeping things feels painful to them. If someone else expresses an interest in something belonging to this type of Fourth Born, the item suddenly becomes precious and vital to the Fourth Born, even if it has been gathering dust in the attic or basement for years.

The same holds true of people for these Fourth Borns. Their partners are really possessions, and they never stop being possessions. One Fourth Born high school girl broke up with her boyfriend and showed no interest in him for almost two years. But when her ex starting dating someone else, this girl decided she wanted him back. To her, he was a possession that no one else could have, even if she didn't really want him.

Fourth Borns who feel this way about their partners often will be drawn to the most attractive person. They may compliment their partners on how good they look; they may even insist that their partners dress a certain way, exercise every day or lose weight so they can keep looking good. It makes sense, from the Fourth Born's point of view. Just as you want your new car to be free from rust, dents, and scratches, you want your other possessions to be in good shape.

To secure a partner, the Fourth Born will be charming, kind, thoughtful and caring. He or she is on a campaign, during courtship, to possess the other person and will do anything to accomplish that. The target of this campaign feels good about the way the Fourth Born acts— may even feel flattered and fortunate that such a wonderful person wants to be part of his or her life.

That can change in an instant with marriage. Once the wedding is over and the marriage license is signed, "ownership" is complete for the

Fourth Born and he can stop trying to make the purchase. (It's important to note that, while we use "he" for convenience here, Fourth Born women can exhibit these same behaviors.) He doesn't have to be a nice guy now; he can let her know that she belongs to him. Many a bride married to this type of Fourth Born man has spent her wedding night in tears because the man she thought she was marrying was not the man she got. The nicest guy in the world has morphed into a nasty, and sometimes dangerous, monster.

This is the type of Fourth Born who will become violent, especially if the partner tries to leave the relationship. The Fourth Born will say something like, "If I can't have you, no one will." They would rather destroy their partners than see someone else enjoy them.

Interestingly, living together without being married can stop this cycle and keep the Fourth Born from regarding his or her partner as a possession. Without the marriage license, there is no "purchase," no "owner" and no "possession," so the relationship can proceed on a more equal footing.

EXERCISE: When we see each other as individuals, we recognize that the other person has rights, just as we do. And when we recognize our partners' rights, it means we are taking responsibility for our relationship rather than taking our partners for granted. Use the following questions about rights to ensure you and your partner are thinking of each other as individuals.

- Does your partner have the right to leave you?
- Does your partner have the right to do what he or she wants?
- Does your partner have the right to go where he or she wants?
- Does your partner have the right to associate with whomever he or she wants?
- Does your partner have the right to believe what he or she wants?
- Does your partner have the right to talk to you the way he or she wants?
- Does your partner have the right to feel the way he or she feels?

When each partner has these same rights and decides to exercise those rights in ways that benefit and strengthen your relationship, you are relating to each other as individuals, not as possessions.

The Fourth Born and the Only

Fourth Borns and Onlies can have a tough time together. Each thinks he understands the other, but in truth they don't have a clue about each other. They're operating from different ends of a spectrum, but they don't realize it.

These two birth orders can seem similar in many respects. The Fourth Born tendency to withdraw in large groups may look like the Only's preference for being alone. But the Fourth Born withdraws because he feels unwanted, not because he wants to be alone. The Only wants to be alone so he won't feel pressured. The Fourth Born's ability to manipulate others' feelings may look like the Only's attempts to "fix" others' feelings. But the Fourth Born uses his abilities to assert control, to get others to do what he wants. The Only fixes others' feelings because he feels what others feel, and he can only feel good if others feel good.

This fundamental disconnect can make life miserable, especially for Onlies paired with angry Fourth Borns. Angry Fourth Borns are most likely to be abusive in their relationships, and common Only behaviors can easily trigger a Fourth Born's anger. For example, Onlies who want to be organized will want to know where their partners are and when to expect them home. Fourth Borns feel they're being treated like children when their partners keep tabs on them, and they often respond angrily. When the Fourth Born gets angry, the Only feels bad and will try to "fix" things so the Fourth Born, and consequently the Only, will feel better. But the Fourth Born gets angry at these efforts because, in the Fourth Born view, grown-ups only try to appease children, not other grown-ups.

Making even relatively simple decisions can be agonizing for the Fourth/Only couple. This is because their thinking patterns are completely different. The Only, who worries when things are left undone, wants to make a decision so he won't have to think about this particular thing anymore; he can't get organized until a decision is made. The Fourth Born, who tries to avoid feeling trapped, wants to take the time to thoroughly analyze every angle and will put off making a decision as long as possible.

Maggie and Tim went through this cycle with the carpet in their house. Tim wanted to get a new carpet; the old one had been in the house since before they were married. But in the four years they were together, Tim and Maggie never could agree on a carpet. Tim, an Only, would ask Maggie what kind of carpet she would like, and Maggie, the Fourth Born, would get angry. No matter how Tim phrased the question, she got angry. Finally, Tim decided to go with her to the store to see what she liked, but that didn't work, either; in the store, Maggie was sullen and uncooperative, refusing even to indicate a preference.

Maggie couldn't decide what kind of new carpet she wanted because she felt she would be trapped as soon as she made a choice. Her analytical mind couldn't stop asking, "What if I find something I like better later on?" Because she couldn't make a choice, Tim couldn't get organized to make sure she was happy, and, as an Only, he was unable to just get what he thought was best.

Even if Tim had chosen new carpeting, Maggie probably would have criticized his decision. This would have made her feel grown-up; by finding fault with him, she would have been able to affirm her own maturity. Tim knew her well enough to anticipate this result, so he did not get a new carpet. He would rather live with the old carpet than with Maggie's criticism.

EXERCISE: Giving in to a Fourth Born can make the Fourth Born angry because he or she feels immature. Although most of us have been conditioned to avoid confrontations if possible, those with Fourth Born partners will find their relationships go more smoothly when they stand up to their partners. This can be done firmly without becoming confrontational by turning an issue into a challenge. For example, Tim would have had better luck with the carpet issue if he had said to Maggie, "Can you help me pick out a new carpet this week?" Once at the carpet store, he could challenge Maggie again, without making her feel trapped: "Can you help me pick out three patterns to consider?" Then, with the samples at home, he could challenge her a third time: "Can you help me decide which one looks better?" By being patient and making each step a challenge, you encourage your Fourth Born partner to help you make decisions without pushing him or her into a corner.

The Fourth Born and the First Born

Fourth Borns and First Borns can have a hard time relating to each other. Fourth Borns want to know what others think and feel so they can analyze them. But First Borns don't know what they think and feel, so they can't help Fourth Borns figure them out. In fact, Fourth Borns might interpret First Born ambivalence as a way of keeping the Fourth Born at arm's length—in other words, the Fourth Born will feel unwanted by the First Born.

Conversely, First Borns don't understand Fourth Born thinking or ideas of justice. If a First Born tries to get a Fourth Born's respect or approval (substitutes for love in the First Born mind) by exerting emotional power, the Fourth Born may slip into "get even" mode, starting a cycle of emotional pain and retaliation for both partners.

Fourth Borns and First Borns can be attracted to each other, sometimes instantly. As a matter of fact, Fourth Borns often are immediately attracted to others, even going so far as determining that they're going to marry a person after only one meeting. This can put other birth orders off, but it is characteristic of the Fourth Born to progress rapidly to emotional intimacy.

Carla and Chuck experienced this instant mutual attraction. Both had been unhappily married before, but they hit it off together beautifully. They decided from the beginning of their relationship not to have sex until they were married. This was Carla's idea; as a Fourth Born, she wanted to avoid being trapped, and she felt that having sex could make her feel trapped. For Chuck, a First Born, it was natural to express his love for Carla by agreeing with her, and this agreement made Carla feel good because it meant he took her feelings seriously. If he had tried to change her mind, she would have felt that he discounted her feelings and probably would have walked away from the relationship.

Because she doesn't feel trapped and because she knows Chuck takes her feelings seriously, Carla is free to express her affection for him. For his part, Chuck feels energized by the love he receives from her, and he feels genuinely loved because Carla takes the initiative in their relationship, rather than waiting for him to decide what to do.

EXERCISE: Fourth Borns want to know what other people want, but First Borns tend to be out of touch with what they want. Fourth Borns can overcome the natural frustration of this situation by telling their partners what they want. For example, instead of asking your First Born partner what's for dinner, tell him or her what you want for dinner. Instead of asking what your partner wants to do this weekend, tell him or her what you'd like to do. You can encourage your partner to express his or her own opinion by saying, "You might not agree with this, but I'd like to go to the planetarium on Saturday." This way, you make your wishes known, and at the same time you give your partner a chance to tell you what he or she thinks.

The Fourth Born and the Second Born

The Fourth Born is a mystery to the Second Born. On the surface, Fourth Born qualities seem familiar to the Second Born, but there is an emotional element that Second Borns don't understand naturally and that can make Fourth Born behavior and logic appear slightly bent, if not actually twisted, to the Second Born.

Second Borns see themselves as being self-disciplined. Fourth Borns talk about trying hard, which sounds like self-discipline. But the Fourth Born makes himself try hard after overcoming an internal emotional struggle—the Fourth Born would rather try hard than appear to be lazy.

The Second Born's self-discipline doesn't come from feelings, it comes from ignoring feelings. The Second Born doesn't understand the emotional component in the Fourth Born's thinking.

In the same way, Fourth Born criticism and Second Born criticism aren't really alike. The Fourth Born criticizes to make himself feel more grown-up. If he can point out the difficulties and flaws in his life, or in those around him, then the Fourth Born is showing that he really is trying hard and, therefore, really is mature. Second Born criticism comes from the desire to achieve perfection, but the Fourth Born doesn't really care about perfection. In fact, to some Fourth Borns, perfection might be undesirable, because if things are perfect, life will be easy, and that doesn't fit in with the Fourth Born's view of what it means to be an adult.

This difference in motivations caused problems for Sam, a Fourth Born, and his wife Terri, a Second Born. Terri was unhappy in their relationship and wanted Sam to get counseling. She didn't go with him; she wanted him to go alone. Sam reported that his wife was very negative, always finding fault with him. This is common for Second Borns who are unable to express their feelings directly; anger will come out in the form of criticism. After Sam learned this about Terri, he tried to make her understand him. But she didn't respond in the way he expected. Instead, she would take what he said and turn it around to find fault again.

Things began to improve when Sam turned his attention away from his own frustration and began thinking about ways to make Terri feel loved. He realized that he often made "I hate . . ." statements about his job, about foods he didn't care for, about the pattern on the wallpaper. These kinds of statements can create a subliminal atmosphere of dislike in our partners, but Fourth Borns like Sam don't intend to make their partners feel unloved when they make these remarks. They are really trying to experience maturity. In his struggle to be grown-up, Sam had to make his environment difficult for himself; in conquering these difficulties, he would feel mature.

The effect of these statements on Terri was devastating. Sam's comments didn't include any suggestions for improvement, which Terri would have welcomed. They were simply complaints. With no idea of how to make things better, Terri felt inadequate and frustrated, and she released her bad feelings by finding fault with Sam. As Sam worked on making more "I love ..." statements and fewer "I hate ..." statements, their ability to enjoy each other improved.

EXERCISE: Sometimes, Fourth Borns interpret Second Born criticism as an attempt to assign blame, and that's a source of anger for Fourth Borns. The Fourth Born can break this cycle by telling the Second Born, "This may not be perfect, but ..." The Second Born can short-circuit the Fourth Born's anger by saying, "This is the way I want it. Can you do that for me?" Again, making something into a challenge allows the Fourth Born to feel mature; clearly stating what you want and sticking to it gives the Fourth Born a sense of security because he or she doesn't have to re-analyze what you want.

The Fourth Born and the Third Born

This can be an awkward relationship from the start. Fearless Third Borns may try to exert emotional power too often for the Fourth Born's comfort, while the passivity of the fearful Third Born can make the Fourth Born feel immature. The Third Born's tendency to rescue others can also exacerbate the Fourth Born's feelings of never being able to grow up.

Fourth Born manipulation will make a Third Born feel vulnerable, and this is so uncomfortable for the Third Born that often he or she will walk away from the relationship. Third Borns also won't respond well to the Fourth Born's efforts to avoid feeling trapped, because many times these efforts translate into unpredictable behavior that don't give the Third Born any opportunity to feel safe.

George, a Fourth Born, felt trapped in his marriage with Rachel, a Third Born. He spent years trying to figure out how he could leave the relationship. Eventually, Rachel accepted the fact that George didn't want to be married to her, so she decided to get on with her life and let George go his own way. As soon as Rachel made this decision, George decided he didn't want the marriage to end. Because Rachel was ready to let him go, George no longer felt trapped and he could stay in the relationship; in fact, he didn't understand why Rachel wanted out. Although George went to counseling and tried to win Rachel back, she refused to reconcile with him. His lack of loyalty had made her feel vulnerable, and she wasn't willing to risk that again. She wasn't interested in finding out why George had acted the way he did, especially because she had done nothing in the first place to contribute to his feeling of being trapped.

EXERCISE: Third Borns tend to care about others more than themselves, and Fourth Borns can give their Third Born partners many opportunities to care about them. By expressing how you feel, you allow your Third Born to sympathize with you and to demonstrate his or her affection by helping. Simple, direct phrases are best: "I'm nervous about going to the party." "I feel like eating out tonight." "I feel tired." "I feel like getting away for a few days." "I would like a new suit for the wedding."

As you practice telling your Third Born partner how you feel, you'll find that he or she finds more ways to make you feel loved, cared for, and wanted.

The Fourth Born and Other Fourth Borns

Fourth Borns don't seem to get together very often. They fear being trapped themselves, but they'll use strategies to trap others. In dating, two Fourth Borns will be aware of the traps the other is trying to set, and they tend to dance around each other rather than with each other. However, Fourth Borns can get together under special circumstances, such as working side by side at similar jobs. Because Fourth Borns tend to be wary of other people, they have to take time to get used to the idea of being together before considering marriage.

When two Fourth Borns do connect, they understand each other's sense of humor, analytical turn of mind, and need for hard work. But communication can be very difficult. Fourth Borns tend to withdraw into themselves when things get tough, so two Fourth Borns who are having problems may not talk to each other for days or weeks on end, which can leave both feeling unwanted.

Nick and Donna fell into this pattern. Their relationship wasn't turbulent, but they couldn't seem to get the lines of communication open, so they couldn't solve problems together. When things got difficult, they'd just stop talking altogether, and when they did speak they'd both present themselves with their arms folded across their chests. They simply weren't open to each other. Each waited for the other to make a decision, but neither one would for fear of becoming trapped. Their relationship was a stalemate; unable to communicate, they couldn't push their marriage from "tolerable" to "good."

EXERCISE: Nonverbal communication is important in any relationship, but it's especially important between Fourth Borns because Fourth Borns analyze nonverbal clues to figure out what the other person is thinking. Closed body language—leaning away from the other person, folding your arms across your chest, little or no eye contact—is one way of showing that you aren't open to the other person. When you and your partner have a tough issue to resolve, opening up your body language will help you communicate. Start with, "Can we talk about this?" Then make sure your arms are at your sides and that you make eye contact with each other. If your partner is still using closed body language, call it to his or her attention by saying, "Can you listen for a moment?" This should trigger more open body language, which will enhance your verbal communication.

Communication—or lack of it—is one of the most common problems in marriage. In the next chapter, we take a close look at the five stages of communication and how each Birth Order Personality approaches communication differently.

CHAPTER EIGHT

The Birth Order Effect and Communication

There's a very old joke about two deaf gentlemen in a train in England. As the train pulls into Wembley Station, the first gentleman says, "This is Wembley."

"No, it's Thursday," says the second gentleman.

"Yes, so am I," replies the first.

What we have here, as the warden in *Cool Hand Luke* would say, is a failure to communicate.

The way we communicate with other people is influenced by how we think of them and how we think of ourselves, and that can change in a heartbeat, depending on what else is going on in our lives and inside our heads. But it also helps to know how each Birth Order Personality tends to communicate; without that knowledge, we may never really understand each other.

There are five stages of communication: greeting, small talk, activity, humor, and intimacy. Not every relationship goes through all these stages; some stop at the humor stage, and others never make it past the greeting. But every close relationship, whether it's with your parents, your siblings, your best friend or your partner, goes through all five stages—over and over and over again.

The first four stages are necessary to achieve the fifth, intimacy. Without the ritual of greeting, there is no initial connection. Without small talk, there is no way to assess the possibility of connecting with each other. Activity is vital for day-to-day living and working together. Humor is necessary to strengthen the connection and move toward intimacy. When you understand these stages and how each Birth Order Personality approaches them, your relationship improves because there are fewer opportunities for miscommunication and the resulting conflict.

Hello, Goodbye

The greeting is the ritual we all engage in dozens of times a day. We say good morning to our families, to our coworkers. We say hello to the delivery guy, to the cashier at the grocery store, to our neighbors, and to the telemarketer who interrupts our dinner. It's an acknowledgment of another person's presence in our lives, however brief. That's why, when we walk down the street in our hometown, we say hello to the people we pass.

At least, those of us who live in smaller communities do that. It's not as common in large metropolitan areas, for a variety of reasons, and it can come as a bit of culture shock when city folk witness this ritual in outlying areas. One New York City native pulled into a parking lot at the University of Iowa one morning. As she got out of her car, a young man got out of his car in the next space, nodded to her and said, "Good morning." She shot him a quizzical glance, said nothing, and walked briskly to her meeting. There, obviously flustered, she told a colleague about the encounter and ended the saga by asking, "What did he mean by that?"

He was just being friendly. He was acknowledging her presence with an innocuous, noncommittal phrase—the way we all do when we're feeling all right with the world.

When we don't feel all right with the world, when we're distracted, or busy, or angry—especially when we're angry—the greeting is the first thing we drop. Omit the greeting, and you can almost feel the tension build in the air around you. Failing to say "hello" to the cashier at the grocery store is a cue that we're not in the mood for chit-chat. Failing to say "good morning" to our partner is a cue that we're upset with him or her. And, believe us, the cashier and the partner both know exactly what it means.

Each Birth Order Personality responds to greetings in its own way. Onlies tend to be enthusiastic in their responses. First Borns are more tentative, reflecting in their own greeting how the other person greeted them. Second Borns tend to be correct in their greetings; you'll seldom hear inappropriate responses from them. Third Borns inject a touch of humor into their greetings. Fourth Borns tend to be brief; they are the most likely to omit the greeting and plunge into activity, humor or even intimacy without going through the preliminary steps.

EXERCISE: For one week, make the time to greet everyone you meet or talk with—colleagues, delivery people, the person who answers the phone on a business call—with a smile and a "Hello, how are you?" Pay attention to the responses you get. You may be surprised at how often this simple, friendly greeting will lead to small talk, and maybe even new friendships.

Nice Day, Isn't It?

Small talk is the way we connect with other people. It gives us a chance to gauge the other person's interests, how he or she feels about things, and what he or she cares about. This also is where we begin paying attention to nonverbal communication—the gestures, facial expressions, vocal inflection, and eye contact—to augment our understanding of the other person's actual words.

The weather is the Number One topic for small talk; in an instant, you can find out whether another person prefers sunshine or rain, hot weather or cold, spring or fall. Current events is the Number Two topic for small talk; by discussing items from the worlds of politics, sports, economics, and even the comics page, we learn more about each other, what we're interested in, what we care about and how we feel.

Small talk isn't always trivial or superficial. We talk about things we've seen on the news, about illness in the family, about problems raising children and getting along with our in-laws. We talk about our fears, our hopes, our losses, and our triumphs. This is how we learn about each other. We connect with each other not just with our words, but with our facial expressions, eye contact, gestures, and tone of voice.

When we make that connection during small talk, whatever the topic, it usually is followed by a pause or ritual of some sort. For instance, if we're chatting with a colleague in the break room, we'll make the connection through small talk, and then we'll say something like, "Well, back to work." If we're on a date, we'll stop chatting and start reading the menu. These things happen naturally, almost as if by some secret but mutually understood signal. That secret signal is the connection. Once we've connected with another person, we subconsciously say to ourselves, "OK, time to move on to the next thing."

When the connection isn't made, or when one of the people involved doesn't sense the connection, the pause following small talk will feel awkward and forced. Have you ever met someone who could small-talk your ear off? This is the coworker who follows you from the break room to your desk, the date who keeps talking while you've got your nose buried in the menu. You're ready to move on to the next thing, but the other person didn't get the message. Most likely, this person is an Only; Onlies have a hard time recognizing when they've connected with other people, so that secret signal often goes by them unnoticed.

First Borns tend to be listeners in small talk, indicating agreement by nodding. Second Borns might offer corrections or criticisms because they tend to listen for mistakes; if you say, for example, that it's supposed to reach seventy degrees today, a Second Born might respond, "Well, Channel Two said sixty-eight this morning." Third Borns will engage in small talk for just so long before they get impatient; they prefer the activity stage. Fourth Borns often take a passive role in small talk because they are listening and watching the speaker to analyze behavior and attitudes.

EXERCISE: For one week, listen to a different radio station in the car, read a different newspaper or watch a different television program. If necessary, make little notes for yourself about the new things you heard, read or saw, then talk about them with your partner. One small paragraph in a weekly newspaper can lead to all kinds of new conversations—and discovering new things about yourself and your partner.

Don't Just Sit There—Do Something!

The activity stage of communication is just what it sounds like. It happens when we work together, think together, and play together. The activity can be anything: tending the garden, playing golf, planning the household budget, choosing a rental movie. Even the most mundane activities offer opportunities for us to relate to each other, if we take advantage of them.

Activity is the heart of dating. Going out to eat, attending a concert, taking a walk—all of these give us an opportunity to see each other in a new light, to find out more about each other, and to strengthen the connection we made during all that small talk. When we talk about married couples "dating," what we're really saying is that they're doing things together so that each partner can continue the journey of discovering more about the other.

Consider the activity of picking out a new carpet for your living room. This can be a wonderful opportunity to relate to your partner, or it can be one of those I-don't-care-whatever-you-want episodes that can drive you crazy. Remember Tim, an Only, and Maggie, a Fourth Born, from Chapter Seven? Their difficulty in buying a carpet was due to their birth order characteristics. Tim looked for hints as to what Maggie would like, while Maggie refused to even express a preference, fearing she would find something she liked better later on. A First Born would be more likely to wait for the partner to make a decision and then go along with it, while a Third Born would be likely to say, "This is your domain, so you do what makes you happy." Second Borns will look for flaws and may put off making a decision because nothing seems close enough to perfect. If you don't understand that these responses come from birth order, it's very difficult to get past them, and it can lead to lots of needless frustration for you and your partner.

But if you bring home the carpet samples, and every night you place them around the furniture in the living room, and you discuss whether this mauve pile clashes with the couch and whether that beige Berber is just too blah for words, then you and your partner are relating to each other. You probably will notice the typical birth order response from your partner, and maybe even from yourself. But now that you know why you and your partner respond the way you do, you can look at the whole carpet-buying issue from a different angle, and you just might find out something new.

EXERCISE: Find ways to turn routine household duties into activities you and your partner can do together. For example, instead of just making out a grocery list, ask your partner to help you plan the dinner menu for the week. When it's time to dust the living room, experiment with rearranging knick-knacks or pictures, and ask your partner for his or her input. You might meet some resistance from your partner, especially if he or she is accustomed to a certain routine; to encourage your partner to participate, use these phrases:

- If your partner is an Only: "Would you help me with this tonight?"
- If your partner is a First Born: "I would appreciate if you would ..."
- If your partner is a Second Born: "Which do you think is better?"
- If your partner is a Third Born: "Would you help me with this, please?"
- If your partner is a Fourth Born: "Can you help me do this?"

Just Kidding!

As one astute observer put it, love may make the world go 'round, but laughter keeps us from getting dizzy.

The humor stage of communication arises naturally out of the activity stage. Whenever we're engaged in an activity, whether at work, at home or out on the town, sooner or later, we'll start cracking jokes. Observe two or more people playing cards or a board game, for example: If all goes well, there should be lots of laughter. If there isn't, something is wrong.

Humor is essential to a healthy relationship. This is why couples who marry always have the same intelligence level. Intelligence isn't the same thing as education; one partner may have a college degree while the other stopped after high school, but that doesn't determine one's intelligence. The partners' intellectual fortes may differ—one may be book smart, and the other may excel in common sense, which is really just applying one's own experience to new situations—but the level of intelligence is the same. It has to be, in order to appreciate each other's sense of humor. It only takes us a short time to gauge another person's intelligence, and that is done through humor. If, on a first date, two people don't understand each other's sense of humor, chances are there won't be a second date. They simply won't be attracted to each other.

Humor adds depth to a relationship by giving us the freedom to be playful. When we're being playful, our other defense mechanisms generally are muted; if we're relaxed enough to make jokes, we're not tense enough to be constantly on our guard.

One First Born man learned how important humor was in relating to his wife. Spurred by a pitiless self-examination that revealed what he considered to be defects in his own behavior, he made a firm resolve to become the perfect husband. He did all the things he thought the perfect husband would do: He fulfilled his obligations, kept his promises, devoted time to his family and to his church. In short, he became a paragon of virtue, steeped in serious purpose.

About three weeks into this self-imposed make over, the man's wife lashed out at him. "You have to stop this," she sobbed. "I can't take it anymore!"

What she couldn't take was the utter lack of humor in the marriage. The First Born had neglected to include laughter in his formula for becoming the perfect husband, and the almost somber attitude he had adopted made his wife desperately unhappy. They had lost that liberating sense of playfulness that makes a relationship fun.

Of course, humor is a delicate thing, and it easily can cause pain. On one level, humor is joking around, enjoying each other. On another, the joking is perceived as serious, and people get angry. Much miscommunication between couples is the result of misunderstanding the partners' sense of humor.

Each Birth Order Personality has its own favorite form of humor. Onlies use sarcasm, changing the meaning of what others say by giving the words a twist. For example, an Only might say, "Sure you want to help me. You just want my money."

A First Born might respond to that by saying, "If I wanted money, I sure wouldn't come to you!" The First Born's humor is pleasantly embarrassing—the kind of thing that might make you blush, followed by a smile or a wink to show that it's humor.

Second Borns use teasing, and they use it on themselves as much as on other people. A typical Second Born would tell the Only, "Of course I want your money. I always want money." Often, the Second Born has to announce that he or she is teasing, because the humor is delivered with a mock seriousness. In this example, the Only might really begin to dig into his pocket if he pays attention to the serious tone of voice and not to the twinkle in the Second Born's eye.

The Third Born's humor usually contains an element of comparison that can be taken as a put-down. A Third Born would tell the Only, "Money? You're the only one I know who's poorer than I am!"

Fourth Born humor goes a step further, using insults to get a smile. A Fourth Born might say, "Well, the only time I can ever get any money out of you is when you need something from me."

Good birth order humor lets each Birth Order Personality respond to the other's particular brand of humor with his or her own. For example, a Fourth Born man greeted his visiting in-laws by saying, "So, you couldn't afford a motel and you have to come sponge off of us?" The brother-in-law, a First Born, replied, "Calm down, you old coot. I'm here to see my sister, not you." Both men laughed; their friendship was affirmed.

Because of the insulting quality of their humor, Fourth Borns are most likely to rub others the wrong way when they use it. Fourth Borns also tend not to respect boundaries, and they often skip the earlier stages of communication, which can lead to misunderstandings. One Fourth Born man approached a minister immediately after a funeral service and asked the minister if he made a lot of money doing funerals. To most people, this would seem inappropriate at best, offensive at worst. But if the minister recognized it as humor, he could have responded in kind; if the minister were a Third Born, for instance, he might have answered, "No, I don't make enough money from funerals. I can hardly wait for yours."

Humor may be the most difficult area to work on, because good humor arises naturally. When it's forced—when we intentionally try to be funny—the humor usually falls flat. But humor can be enhanced when we turn our attention to "play." After all, humor really is an adult form of play. Fortunately, there are all kinds of ways adults can play—card games, bowling, fishing, bicycling—you really are limited only by your hobbies and interests, and those limits apply only if you let them. Even work can count as play, if it's something you enjoy doing with other people.

How can work become play? It happens when we change our attitudes. Attitude is everything in enhancing humor. When we say we "have to" do something, that something becomes a chore. Certainly, there are some things that must be done, if only because we don't want to deal with the consequences of not doing them. But there are many things we want to do because we'll feel better when we've done them. We say we "have to" organize the garage, but the truth is we want to organize the garage so we can find things easily and park the car there. We "have to" stack the firewood, but we really want to do it so we can have a cozy fire in the middle of winter.

Think of the difference this way: When we "have to" do something, we are being pushed by outside forces. "Have to" means it is not our choice, it's someone else's choice, and we are obligated to do it. "Want to," on the other hand, comes from inside. Our own desires make us want to do things; it is our personal choice, and no one else is forcing us to do anything.

Humor is the lubricant that reduces friction in a marriage, smoothing the sharp edges that routinely crop up in daily life. Misunderstood humor is probably the greatest single cause of marital conflict, causing hurt feelings and resentment when the jokes are taken seriously. This kind of misunderstanding can happen in any birth order combination, largely because of the nature of birth order humor. The Second Born's teasing can feel like genuine criticism. The Fourth Born's insults are often spoken so seriously that the recipient doesn't recognize them as humor. First Borns tend to feel guilty after using their shaming type of humor and might apologize immediately to make sure the other person doesn't take offense. Third Born put-downs are usually delivered with a smile, but sometimes can be misconstrued. The Only Child's sarcasm does not seem to cause much trouble; although no one understands the Only (except another Only), their humor seems to be easily recognizable by all the birth order personalities.

EXERCISE: Flag the words "have to" in conversation with your partner. Ask your partner to point it out when you say "have to," and do the same for your partner. When you catch each other saying "have to," ask, "Do you really have to, or do you want to?" By breaking the "have to" habit, you'll be able to find enjoyment—and humor—in more of the things you do.

Two Hearts That Beat as One

You know the old saying, "A friend is someone who knows everything about you—and likes you anyway." That's intimacy, the fifth stage of communication and, often, the hardest for us to get to. It's where the fences come down, the pretenses are shed, and we accept each other for the incredible beings we are, flaws and all. We're not talking about physical intimacy. We're talking about that sense of closeness that comes when we're relating directly to the other person; when we're not using small talk, an activity or humor to connect. Intimate communication often doesn't even involve words. It's just being with that other person and being comfortable there.

In intimate moments, every Birth Order Personality sets aside his or her coping skills. Onlies are no longer in their own world. First Borns are themselves, not trying to impress. Second Borns are in touch with their own feelings. Third Borns feel safe. Fourth Borns feel wanted.

True intimacy is a rare treat to be savored. It can be broken by outside forces—the telephone ringing, for example—or by ourselves. Humor will shatter an intimate moment because jokes reestablish distance. If you make a joke during an intimate moment and the other person isn't ready to let go of the intimacy, be prepared for this familiar rebuke: "Does everything have to be a joke with you? Can't you be serious for one minute?"

Intimate communication means we see the other person as a real human being and we are relating to that real human being. This is where it gets tricky for each of the birth order personalities, because each has its own way of de-personalizing other people. It's part of each birth order's coping skills, and those skills have to be set aside to achieve real intimacy.

When the Only isn't relating to others as persons, he or she sees others as Things that need fixing. Remember, Onlies staved off loneliness in childhood by creating imaginary friends and they continue that habit into adulthood. When they don't see others as individual people, Onlies imagine what others are feeling and thinking, and if others don't conform to that imaginary picture, Onlies will try to "fix" them until they do.

First Borns see other people as Judges who can condemn the First Born and therefore must be placated. When First Borns de-personalize other people this way, they will delay offering an opinion or making a decision until they think they've figured out what others want, or they will charge ahead trying to impress others so they will be judged with approval.

Second Borns de-personalize others by viewing them as Projects that need to be perfected. In this mode, Second Borns will respond favorably to people who indicate they want to do better; in fact, Second Borns are remarkably accepting of incompetence in other people, as long as those other people "are trying to do better." On the other hand, people who are competent but show little or no interest in improvement can annoy the Second Born to no end, and eventually the Second Born will discard these Projects.

Third Borns view others as Victims who need to be rescued. Third Borns relate best when others need help, and they may not know how to relate to someone when that person does not need help. For Third Borns to treat others as persons, they have to figure out how to get out of rescuing mode.

For Fourth Borns who aren't relating to people as real human beings, others are Possessions to be controlled. As children, Fourth Borns had to work hard to keep their older siblings from taking their things away. As adults, Fourth Borns still work hard to keep control over their things, and that behavior often plays out in their interactions with other people.

In a healthy relationship, intimacy ebbs and flows like the tide. Like humor, intimacy cannot be forced; it must be allowed to develop in a natural rhythm within a relationship. But you can enhance intimacy with your partner by remembering to relate to him or her as an individual and by regularly focusing your thoughts on what you like about your partner and your relationship.

EXERCISE: Learning to enjoy silence can enhance intimacy with your partner. This can be difficult; most people find silence uncomfortable and will try to fill it with words or activity. To overcome this discomfort, try this exercise at least once a week in short periods, no longer than five minutes at first. If necessary, use an egg timer (in another room if possible, so the ticking sound doesn't distract you). Turn off the television, the stereo, and the ringer on the phone. Sit with your partner in a comfortable place—on the couch or in comfortable chairs facing each other. You don't have to maintain eye contact, but do hold hands; this physical connection will help you focus. For the time you've agreed on, think about your partner: what you find attractive in him or her; how his or her hand feels in yours; what you know about his or her dreams and needs. Don't talk during this time. When time is up, smile at each other and do whatever comes next naturally—whether it's cleaning the kitchen or picking up the newspaper. If you and your partner want to discuss what you thought about during the exercise, that's fine, but you don't have to. The point is to help you feel comfortable just being with each other. The more often you do this exercise, the more natural it will feel. With time, you'll find yourself becoming more aware of intimate moments that aren't staged—riding in the car or a mutual glance across the room at a party—and you'll be able to enjoy these moments more.

What Did You Mean by That?

We all know, from painful experience, that there are times when we just don't communicate well with anybody. We misinterpret humor, or our own humor is misinterpreted. We take things seriously when we shouldn't, and vice versa. Sometimes, we misread, or simply miss, nonverbal cues that could tell us more about what another person really means, and sometimes our signals are missed or misread. Sometimes, we wish other people could just read our minds, so we wouldn't have to find the right words, in the right order, and in the right tone of voice, to express what we need to express.

All that is normal, from time to time. Recognizing those times, and being able to accept the fact that they happen to everyone occasionally, takes some practice, just as real, effective communication takes practice. No communication problem is permanent, and no one communication strategy will work all the time. But now you have better tools to understand yourself and your partner, so those times when you simply can't understand each other will come along less and less frequently.

EXERCISE: Communication can be a problem for all the birth orders because of the wide range of meanings we can attach to what others say. We can put meanings into others' words that are far different from what was intended, and that can lead to unnecessary conflict. This exercise is designed to help you and your partner discuss your own interpretations of various phrases so you can better understand the true meaning behind each other's words. You can use the following statements or any others that you choose.

Explain to each other what each statement means to you. There are no right or wrong interpretations, so it's OK for you to have different interpretations of the same statement. Listen to each other and discuss the differences in meaning that you discover. The goal of this exercise is to promote better understanding, which can lead to negotiation, accommodation, and fewer misunderstandings.

- It's time to figure this out.
- I'm not comfortable doing that.
- Do I have to?
- Would you pick up some bread on the way home?
- I just want some time to relax when I get home.
- I don't know what I want to do tomorrow night.
- What do you think about getting a new recliner?
- What are your plans for the weekend?
- Let's go out tonight.
- I feel guilty.
- I need you to move that chair.
- You left a mark on the coffee table.
- You look better in dark blue.
- Your hair needs combing.
- Take your shoes off.
- Don't worry about it.
- I've got an idea.
- That doesn't bother me.
- I'll take care of it.

- I wish you would do something for me.
- You never listen.
- What am I supposed to do?
- You don't know how hard I work.
- We haven't been invited.
- You know what I told you about that.

Now that you know the stages of communication and a little bit about how individual birth order personalities move through those stages, it should be easier to identify the communication patterns in your own relationship and to try new strategies to keep the lines of communication clear and functioning. Even during the inevitable rough spots that occur in every marriage, you and your partner may find yourselves asking each other, "What do you mean?" instead of jumping to conclusions!

CHAPTER NINE

The Birth Order Effect and Conflict Resolution

No matter how well you and your partner understand each other's birth order personalities, no matter how compatible the two of you are, no matter how clear your communication, there are going to be some difficult times in your relationship. There may be financial hardships when the economy loses steam. Health issues can put an enormous burden on a relationship, as can other family members. Raising children is always fertile ground for challenging times. Career changes, going back to school, a death in the family—there are so many avenues for stress, anxiety, and frustration to enter our lives that sometimes it's a wonder we don't crumble under the weight.

We can't help you avoid those difficult times, but we can give you information and some tools to help see you through them.

Life Passages

Life is full of milestones. We take our first steps. We go on our first date. We get old enough to drive, old enough to vote, old enough to drink. We get done with school, start a career, get married, have children and start marking their milestones.

But some of the milestones we pass aren't as clearly marked, though they are fully as important—and as long-ranging in their effects—as the easy-to-see ones. We call these less obvious milestones "life passages." These are the times when we experience a sea change in our lives and the way we view the world. Sometimes, these changes are so gradual and occur over such a long period that we don't even realize the tide has shifted. Sometimes, so much else is going on at the same time that we just don't notice.

One of these life passages occurs around age twelve. This is when we begin valuing our friends more than our parents, when we'd rather spend our time away from home than with our families. Another occurs around age sixteen, when we begin to become psychologically independent from our parents. This is often when we rebel in both thoughts and actions; we may date people our parents disapprove of, wear clothes they hate, and listen to music they can't stand, just to assert our individuality.

There are two adulthood life passages that can have a profound impact on relationships. One begins at age twenty-six or so and usually lasts one to two years. This is when most of us truly "grow up," in the sense that we begin to take responsibility for our own lives. Until this point, most people tend to cling to a belief in magic, a sense that everything will somehow work itself out and life will be OK. But as we approach our twenty-sixth birthday, we begin to understand that we have to do things for ourselves. Instead of waiting for things to change, we begin to insist that things change. And we begin to look for ways to achieve the changes we want to make. Many marriages seem to break up when the partners are in their late twenties, and this can be attributed in part to the life passage at age twenty-six. Most people will spend about two years at this point in their lives trying to make the relationship work; if the required changes aren't made by about age twenty-eight, they decide the marriage isn't going to work and they're ready to leave it.

Another life passage occurs at around age thirty-eight—popularly known as "the mid-life crisis." It's really a transition period in which our values about our lives change. If we have devoted our adult lives to being successful in our careers, we may start to value our relationships over our bank balances. If we were carefree and unfettered in our twenties and early thirties, we may begin to feel it's time to settle down and get serious about our lives. It's as if the personality gets folded inside out at age thirty-eight. What was on the back burner now takes precedence, and the things that mattered so much to us before aren't quite so crucial now.

The "crisis" in this life passage comes when the transition is extreme. This is when you find men abandoning their careers—and sometimes their families—to become scuba instructors in Bermuda, or women donning leather miniskirts and listening to Rusted Root. From the outside, these drastic measures can look like pathetic attempts to turn back the clock. But from the inside, it's another shift in the tide.

This shift is easier on a marriage if the partners are close in age; if they go through this life passage more or less at the same time, the relationship can actually improve. Take the example of a man who has been less than responsible, while his wife has carried the load. This has kept the relationship stable over the years. When they reach thirty-eight, he becomes more responsible, while she shifts into a more relaxed mode. The relationship remains stable and in fact is even more balanced than it was before.

If there's a big age difference, say five years or more, the transitions of this life passage can be much more stressful for both partners. In our example above, the man at age thirty-eight begins taking more responsibility, but his wife, thirty-three, is still in the do-it-herself mode. She doesn't understand her "new, improved" husband and may even feel resentful because she doesn't know what she's supposed to do now that's he taking all this responsibility. To him, she seems unreasonable; he's doing now what he should have been doing all along, so why should that be a problem? She's five years away from her own sea change and therefore five years away from understanding the change in him.

For the five birth order personalities, the changes at age thirty-eight can be both dramatic and liberating. The Only Child goes from retreating into his or her own world to enjoying the real world. The First Born goes from looking for respect, approval, and admiration to valuing love. The Second Born goes from ignoring feelings to paying attention to them, especially his or her own feelings. The Third Born goes from seeking security to taking risks in relating with others. The Fourth Born goes from being secretive to being open.

EXERCISE: Communication is at its most vulnerable during times of stress because our feelings interfere with our ability to listen. Listening is thinking about what the other person is saying—not thinking about what you are going to say next.

Each Birth Order Personality has its own listening style. Onlies put their own meanings into others' words. First Borns listen well to others, but aren't very good at listening to themselves. Second Borns listen for mistakes, especially in arguments. Third Borns interpret the intent behind the words. Fourth Borns listen to others or to themselves, but not at the same time.

When you feel your partner slipping into his or her habitual listening style, try these phrases to bring your partner's attention back to truly listening.

- If your partner is an Only: "That's not what I mean. Pay attention to what I'm saying."
- If your partner is a First Born: "You might not agree, but ..."
- If your partner is a Second Born: "This might not be perfect, but ..."
- If your partner is a Third Born: "Please listen to what I'm saying."
- If your partner is a Fourth Born: "This might be hard for you to believe, but ..."

You Made Your Bed, Now Lie in It

All of us have heard this phrase from our parents, our grandparents, perhaps even our siblings or our spouses. Maybe we've even used it with our children. The idea behind this admonition is to teach us about responsibility and accepting the consequences of our actions. But it can have the unfortunate side effect of making us feel trapped, even when we don't want to feel trapped. In the extreme, having to "lie in the bed we made" can lead to commitment phobia.

Commitment phobia can show up early in a marriage—the first few years, or even the first few months. The person with commitment phobia feels trapped and thus is compelled to keep one foot outside the relationship. Both men and women can suffer from commitment phobia, although it appears to be more common in men.

The most usual manifestation of commitment phobia is extramarital sex. Often these are one-night stands rather than ongoing affairs, and often they will occur even when there aren't any problems in the marriage relationship. In fact, the person with commitment phobia can feel even more trapped when the marriage is stable; there isn't any excuse under those circumstances to escape the relationship.

There are other, non-sexual manifestations of commitment phobia. The person who is away from home every weekend—hunting, fishing, attending sporting events—may suffer from commitment phobia. Being away from home on the weekends can alleviate the feeling of being trapped. People who put relationships with their parents or siblings ahead of their relationships with their spouses may do so because of commitment phobia.

This is, of course, extreme behavior. It is normal for people to want some time apart from their spouses. Our relationships, like our bodies, need room to breathe; we need time to be apart as much as we need time to be close. When we are uncomfortable at even the prospect of being close, that's when we have trouble with commitment. That's when we don't want to lie in the bed we made.

The up side of all this is that, by learning about birth order and how it affects our relationships, we don't have to escape from the beds we've made. If we don't like them, we can remake them.

EXERCISE: We all need to get away occasionally. That's why we have coffee breaks, weekends, and vacations. In relationships, our getaways take the form of lunch dates with friends, hobbies, volunteer work, and so on. But each Birth Order Personality attaches a different feeling to time away from a spouse.

Onlies relish time by themselves; they may even wake earlier than the rest of the household or stay up after everyone else has gone to bed so they can have an hour or two to themselves each day. If your Only partner seems unusually cranky or tense, lack of alone time might be the cause. When this happens, encourage your partner to take some time on his or her own; if that means rearranging a schedule, show your partner how the schedule will work so he or she can get reorganized.

First Borns have a harder time getting away. If their spouses want time without them, First Borns may feel guilty, thinking they've offended their partners. But if First Borns do something without their partners, they may feel guilty about leaving their partners out. To encourage your First Born partner to explore time away from you, let him or her know that you approve of the activities you aren't involved in. You might even say, for example, "I want you to go to lunch with your friends." This express instruction allows the First Born to feel like he or she is pleasing you, so he or she doesn't have to feel guilty about not including you.

Second Borns who are torn between time with their spouses and time away are apt to feel inadequate because they can't satisfy both needs perfectly. Let your Second Born partner know that perfection isn't necessary by saying, "This schedule may not be perfect, but we can work with it." This lets the Second Born know that a reasonable balance between time with you and time away from you is both doable and acceptable.

Third Borns don't like to spend time away from their partners because they feel like they're letting their partners down; if they aren't there to take care of things, to rescue their partners, Third Borns feel weak and therefore unlovable. To counter this feeling, ask your Third Born to spend time with his or her friends, pursuing hobbies, and so on. Saying, for example, "Please call Joe and find out when you can go fishing," lets the Third Born feel that he will please you by doing this.

Fourth Borns tend to feel unwanted, so encouraging your Fourth Born partner to spend time away from you can be tricky. If you try any of the phrases we offered for other birth orders, your Fourth Born will likely become suspicious, thinking you don't want him or her around. Tackle this natural suspicion by saying, "This might be hard for you to believe, but I really want you to take that painting course you've been talking about." You also can put it as a challenge: "Making the time to take that painting course might be hard. Do you think you can do it?" The challenge helps the Fourth Born feel mature by acknowledging the hard work he or she will have to put in.

Special vs. Important

Conflict can also arise in our relationships when we see ourselves as special, rather than important. It's a key distinction, because it changes both our behavior and our expectations.

People who see themselves as special will take rather than give. They love themselves more than others; they want to possess their partners rather than meet their partners' needs. People who see themselves as important, on the other hand, serve. They set aside their own wants and needs to meet the needs of others.

At times, each of us is special, and that's healthy. We're special on our birthdays, for example. On Mother's Day, Mom is special, and on Father's Day, Dad is special. When we receive a service from someone, we're special, and the person providing the service is important; when we're in the hospital, for instance, we're special, and the nurses and doctors and orderlies are important. If your job is a service-oriented one, you are important and the customer or client is special. In working relationships, both people are important; the boss can be important or special, depending on the circumstances.

In healthy personal relationships, parents are important to their children, and children are special to their parents. In a healthy marriage, both partners are important, and occasionally each will be special. Problems crop up when the special/important relationship is skewed. In abusive relationships, the abuser is always special, taking from the abused, wanting to possess the abused, while the abused is always important, trying to meet the abuser's needs while ignoring his or her own needs.

Each Birth Order Personality has its own way of being special and its own way of being important, and these patterns are learned early in childhood from parents and siblings.

The special Only demands order. He won't tolerate anyone else moving his things or leaving their own things lying around; she will explode in anger when she's interrupted. The special Only wants the protection of his or her own world and cannot deal with the intrusion of others. For women, the special attitude may stem from constant approval from the father as a girl, or from feeling superior to the mother; for men, it stems from constant approval from the mother or from feeling superior to the father.

The important Only wants his or her partner to feel good and will take on the responsibility of making sure that happens. The important Only's success in this endeavor depends on the skills he or she has developed.

The special First Born demands respect in lieu of love. At home this means domination, an insistence on obedience to the First Born and agreement with his or her decisions. Disobedience and disagreement mean disrespect to the special First Born, and since respect is a substitute for love, the special First Born won't tolerate disobedience or disagreement. First Borns tend to develop the special attitude when they have a Second Born sibling of the same sex.

The important First Born generally has a Second Born sibling of the opposite sex and learns to look out for others. The important First Born wants to work with his or her partner, to satisfy the partner's needs. Instead of demanding respect, the important First Born seeks approval through cooperation.

The special Second Born has a First Born sibling of the same sex and learns to compete with the older child. The special Second Born looks for ways to dethrone others, to outdo them, to find fault with them.

The important Second Born is a problem-solver and peacemaker. With a First Born sibling of the opposite sex, the important Second Born takes on more responsibility in the family and, instead of competing, looks for ways to make things run smoothly.

The Third Born becomes special with a Second Born sibling of the opposite sex because, in this dynamic, the older child makes the Third Born feel special. In adulthood, special Third Borns demand that their partners make them feel secure. If the special Third Born is angry, he or she will attack the partner for any feelings of insecurity he or she experiences.

The Third Born becomes important when the Second Born sibling is of the same sex. The Third Born is driven to prove his or her fearlessness, and that translates into serving others. These Third Borns are the ones who rescue victims; they are offering, not taking, a service, so they are important rather than special.

The special Fourth Born was treated as special by older siblings of the opposite sex. The special Fourth Born desperately needs attention and will pursue it aggressively. Sometimes, special Fourth Borns will get angry at being left out, at not getting attention, or even at not being talked to or looked at in the right way.

The important Fourth Born has a Third Born sibling of the same sex and didn't get treated as special by the Third Born as a child. This Fourth Born doesn't demand attention; he or she gives it, becoming a buddy to spouse and children, coworkers, and underlings.

A skewed special/important relationship foments continual discontent for the special spouse and ever-growing resentment and anger for the important spouse. As in the Drama Triangle we discussed in Chapter Two, it is impossible for two people to relate to each other on an equal footing if one is always special and the other is always important.

EXERCISE: The balance between special and important is a delicate one, and it's easy to fall into a routine of being one or the other all or most of the time. This exercise will help you measure the special/important balance in your relationship. Fold a sheet of paper in half lengthwise. On one side, write at the top, "Times when I give to others." On the other side, write, "Times when I take from others." List all the things you can think of under each heading. For example, if you do most of the cooking in your house, that would go under the "Times when I give ..." heading. If your partner does most of the cooking, it would go under "Times when I take ..." When you've finished your lists, compare the number of items under each heading. If your lists are relatively balanced, that indicates your relationships have a healthy give-and-take pattern. If you have lots of items under "Times when I give ..." and few under "Times when I take ...," that may be an indication that your needs and wants are pushed aside too often. If you have many items under "Times when I take ..." and few under "Times when I give ...," that can indicate you expect others to take responsibility for satisfying your needs and wants. In either case, examine the items under each heading and ask yourself whether you would be more relaxed, more satisfied or more in tune with your partner if some of those items were modified or dropped entirely.

Seeing Red

All of us get angry now and then. Sometimes it's nothing more than mild irritation; sometimes it's a volcano of fury. Sometimes we get embarrassed about losing our tempers, and other times we feel like we have no choice. And when we're on the receiving end of someone else's anger, sometimes we don't have any idea what it's all about.

One thing to remember is that anger means different things to different birth order personalities.

- When an Only Child expresses anger, it is to let others know how the Only feels. Onlies don't use anger to influence others; they use it to vent.
- First Borns express anger to gain respect or agreement—often after all other attempts have failed.

- Second Borns express anger as a cover for hurt feelings. Before the explosion, a Second Born will tend to become critical; if that doesn't relieve the Second Born's pent-up feelings, he or she will blow up.

- Third Borns express anger to overcome their feelings of vulnerability. Many Third Borns find it difficult to stand up for themselves without becoming angry, so anger often means the Third Born feels taken advantage of.

- Fourth Borns express anger as a form of intimidation, a way to control others. It works because most of us were conditioned as children to be afraid of someone who is angry.

Likewise, the different birth order personalities respond to confrontation differently. Most of us dislike confrontation—some of us more than others—and most of us have been trained from childhood to avoid confrontation whenever possible. But keep in mind that couples who feel free to disagree with each other are more likely to stay together because they can resolve minor differences instead of letting them fester beneath the surface. In fact, one study found that couples who always avoid arguing are thirty-five percent more likely to divorce. So, to keep your marriage healthy, you can't always avoid confrontations with your partner. But you can understand what's going on during a confrontation.

Confrontations occur when there are at least two strongly opposing forces, ideas, personalities, etc. In marriages and other committed relationships, the dynamics of confrontation—the actions and reactions of you and your partner—depend in large part on birth order. Each Birth Order Personality meets opposition in its own way, and the effect of each method is different depending on the partner's birth order.

The Only Child meets confrontation with an expression of emotion. In children, we'd call these outbursts tantrums, but the adult Only Child does the same thing. Unless there are secondary birth order characteristics that allow the Only Child to use power, authority, persuasion or force, the Only Child has just one weapon in his or her psychological arsenal: expressing feelings. Each of the birth order personalities will meet this kind of confrontation in one of two ways:

- Another Only Child will either understand the outburst or react with his or her own emotional outburst.
- A First Born will feel guilty or get angry, with an urge to use power in response.
- A Second Born will feel inadequate or react with angry criticism.
- A Third Born will feel helpless or use humor.
- A Fourth Born will feel responsible or blame the other.

Under normal circumstances, First Borns tend to be passive, compromising, and agreeable. But when they are pushed, First Borns often meet opposition with power. They may be soft-spoken about it, but there is an unmistakable underlying sense of power, and it may come out in the form of an ultimatum, such as, "Either get a job or move out," or "If you don't bring these grades up, you won't be allowed to drive the car." Here is how the five birth order personalities respond to this kind of confrontation:

- An Only Child will try to cater to the First Born, or he or she may want to escape the situation.
- Another First Born will become awkward in relating to this First Born, or there may be a power struggle between the two.
- A Second Born will discount the First Born's behavior as insignificant or try to intimidate the First Born.
- A Third Born will try to appease the First Born or use anger to try to persuade the First Born.
- A Fourth Born will cave in to the First Born or seek to escape.

When Second Borns reach their limits, they often meet opposition with intimidation. They usually don't threaten physical harm, but they will use other kinds of threats. For example, an unhappy Second Born customer at a department store might threaten to talk to a recalcitrant clerk's supervisor, or a social worker might threaten to place an uncooperative client's children in foster care. Here's what the Second Born will encounter from other birth order personalities:

- An Only Child will either try to do the right thing to make the Second Born feel better or will angrily announce that he or she will not take it anymore (without necessarily doing anything beyond this announcement).
- A First Born will be completely defeated and will try to satisfy the Second Born, or he or she will slide into depression.
- Another Second Born will either discount the intimidation tactics or attempt intimidation in return, with the better intimidator ultimately winning.
- A Third Born either will laugh off the intimidation or withdraw.
- A Fourth Born will go along with the Second Born or use his or her analytical reasoning to defeat the Second Born.

Third Borns meet opposition with persuasion. This is one of the reasons Third Borns make such good salespeople. They are able to overcome objections, even a flat-out "no," with persistent persuasion. Because the other birth order personalities are the way they are, Third Borns often come out on the winning side in confrontations.

- An Only Child will go along with the Third Born or react emotionally to the Third Born's arguments.
- A First Born will feel compelled to acquiesce to the Third Born or else leave.
- A Second Born will go along with the Third Born, albeit reluctantly, or react with angry criticism.
- Another Third Born understands the persuasion and may use persuasion of his or her own in response.
- A Fourth Born will feel overcome by the persuasion or become devious to defeat the Third Born.

Fourth Borns meet opposition with force—psychological, physical or both. Fourth Borns who carry a lot of anger are most likely to be physically violent. Psychological force is something the Fourth Born learned as a child in dealing with older siblings; in many cases, this was the only way the Fourth Born could make his or her presence felt. Here's how the other birth order personalities typically respond in confrontation with a Fourth Born:

- An Only Child may try to do things the way the Fourth Born wants them done or may issue a warning that further use of force will end the relationship.
- A First Born will either go along with the Fourth Born or issue an ultimatum.
- A Second Born will focus on doing what the Fourth Born wants or try to intimidate the Fourth Born.
- A Third Born will not let the Fourth Born's behavior bother him or her, or will use persuasion to try to change the Fourth Born's behavior.
- Another Fourth Born will either stop talking to this Fourth Born for days or even weeks or despair of the relationship altogether.

It's normal to have some confrontation in any relationship and especially in a long-term committed relationship like marriage. In a healthy relationship, each partner is free to disagree with the other, and if it's OK to disagree, it's OK to work together to resolve the issue at hand. Disagreements even give us an opportunity to strengthen our bond because they allow us to see things from the other person's perspective and learn more about our partners.

EXERCISE: Although disagreements can arise from many sources, each Birth Order Personality has its own particular trigger for getting angry. Knowing what those triggers are helps you avoid anger when you can and anticipate it when you can't; knowing how to confront the anger helps you diffuse it.

- Onlies become angry when they feel intruded upon—a sudden change in plans or an unexpected obligation that keeps the Only from doing something fun, for example. Confront the Only's anger with: "You can be angry if you want, but ..."
- First Borns become angry when they perceive a lack of respect from others. Confront the First Born's anger with: "I want you to ..."
- Second Borns become angry when they are criticized and will respond with criticism of their own. Confront the Second Born's anger with: "Do you have any other criticisms?"
- Third Borns become angry at being put down. Confront the Third Born's anger with: "I'm disappointed that you ..."
- Fourth Borns become angry when they feel they are being blamed. Confront the Fourth Born's anger with: "Stop it! It's like this ..."

You've learned about birth order, about communication, and about conflict. Now it's time to put the whole package together so you can begin improving your relationship.

CHAPTER TEN

Putting the Birth Order Effect to Work for You

Y̶ou've read the book, you've done the exercises, and you've talked birth order with your partner. You've got all this information and all this insight, but what are you supposed to do with it?

Our hope is that you will enjoy it. One of the cool things about understanding birth order is that it gives us a new perspective on ourselves and the people in our lives. When we understand that our own behaviors are based on our birth order personalities and the coping strategies we developed as children, we can look at ourselves more objectively. We are free to understand how and why we are the way we are without feeling ashamed, guilty, inadequate, depressed or angry. That objectivity allows us to identify the things we like and the things we don't like so much; and then we can figure out ways to adapt those things we don't like to make the changes we want to make in our lives.

Looking at our partners through the prism of birth order also gives us more objectivity. Without knowledge of birth order, our partners can seem unreasonable, purposely irritating, unwilling to change, obnoxious, stubborn, and simply beyond understanding; and we can seem all these things to our partners! The power of birth order is that it allows us to interpret behavior correctly. It shows us that the Second Born's correction is really an expression of love, not of dissatisfaction; that the Fourth Born's insults really are humor, not serious criticisms; that the Only's need for time apart is not a sign of unhappiness in the relationship; that the First Born's daydreaming is really part of the quest for affection; that the Third Born's anger really comes from feelings of being unlovable. Couples who understand each other through birth order are able to communicate with each other, to express and receive love, to laugh together, and to accept each other's coping mechanisms in difficult times.

Of course, birth order is not the only ingredient in a strong, stable, and satisfying relationship. Happy couples relate to each other as individuals, not as Things, Judges, Projects, Victims or Possessions. Happy couples are not hampered by emotional attachments to previous relationships; they have learned how to balance their special-versus-important roles; they recognize difficult times as temporary issues, not permanent roadblocks. In short, these couples have bonded with each other, and they nurture that bond throughout their relationships.

Bonding presents unique challenges for each Birth Order Personality. Onlies are the least likely to feel the need to bond; they are comfortable and content in their own worlds, where their imagination bonds them to things and people. Onlies also tend not to do the things that promote bonding. They don't like to make plans too far in advance because they don't know whether they'll feel like doing something when the time comes. They like to spend time alone, so they don't pursue opportunities to spend time with other people. And, because they can easily imagine how their partners think and feel (even if what they imagine is wrong), Onlies tend to believe that they don't need to bond.

First Borns face a different challenge in bonding. If they are focused on impressing other people or getting their approval—substitutes for love in the First Born world—First Borns can't drop their guard enough to bond. They tend to go along with their partners' wishes in order to please them, rather than getting in touch with what they want themselves; so opportunities to make a true connection are limited.

For Second Borns, the difficulty in bonding comes from their feelings of inadequacy and their preference for logic over emotion. Second Borns may be hesitant to try new things, especially if there aren't clear instructions or steps to follow, because their inexperience hinders their ability to be perfect. They may be critical of suggestions for activities that promote bonding, or they may deny the need to bond because bonding necessarily means making an emotional connection.

Bonding also means being vulnerable, and this is where Third Borns have trouble. Although Third Borns are fairly free in expressing their emotions, they tend to avoid situations where others could use that emotional connection to hurt them. They keep most people at arm's length, allowing themselves to get close to only a select few. Their "it doesn't bother me" defense erects a natural barrier to bonding until they feel safe enough with another person to lower that barrier.

Fourth Borns tend to be suspicious of others, which also inhibits bonding. They may turn down invitations because they don't believe others really want them around, or they may suspect a hidden agenda behind the invitation. Even when they accept such invitations, Fourth Borns may be quiet and withdrawn during the activity or event— another manifestation of their distrust and feelings of being unwanted. They may also shy away from bonding because they fear they'll be trapped.

This is not to say that bonding is impossible, or even necessarily difficult, for couples of any birth order. Most couples have established a bond with each other despite the challenges our birth order personalities present. But many couples, particularly those who have been together for a long time, figure the bond they established at the beginning of their relationship doesn't need any more attention. Too often, once-strong connections gradually weaken; and sometimes they disappear altogether.

EXERCISE: The following questions will help you evaluate the strength of the bond in your relationship. Some of the questions may seem obvious, but they are nonetheless important; if we don't ask ourselves these questions, it's too easy to just plod along without knowing whether our relationship (or our life) is really what we want. You may want to make a few copies of this exercise for future use because bonding is an ongoing process, and it doesn't hurt to check your progress every now and then.

As you go through this worksheet, consider the questions carefully and be as honest as you can in your answers. Remember, this is an assessment to help you determine the level of bonding between you and your partner and identify opportunities for more bonding.

1. Does your partner make you feel good?
2. Do you pay attention to your partner's nonverbal communication?
3. Do you understand your partner's nonverbal communication most of the time?
4. Do you and your partner still go on dates? If so, do you do a variety of activities on your dates, or do your dates have a routine (always dinner and a movie, for example)?
5. How often do you engage in behavior that hinders bonding? For example, using drugs or alcohol impairs your ability to read and interpret nonverbal communication; likewise, if every date ends in sex, the physical aspect of your relationship is taking energy away from the bonding process.
6. If you and your partner live together, do you each have time alone, away from each other? Do you have time together away from home?
7. Are there danger signs in your relationship? If so, you may want to seek professional counseling.
8. Women, did you have a bad relationship with your mother when you were a child? Men, did you have a bad relationship with your father? Those of us who had these bad relationships tend to recreate them with our partners.

9. Are you still hurting from a previous relationship? Those emotions get in the way of bonding with your new partner.
10. When you first met your partner, did you dislike him or her? That feeling is apt to rise again at some point in your relationship.
11. Are you putting up with your partner now, hoping he or she will change? If so, things will get worse, not better, as the relationship progresses.
12. Do your friends worry about your relationship? They may see something you don't.

No Talking, Please

Bonding is the ability to "read" each other's nonverbal communication—facial expressions, body language, gestures, tone of voice, and so on. According to one study, as much as ninety-three percent of all our communication is made through these nonverbal means. If you can't read your partner's nonverbal communication, imagine how much you're missing!

We learn what others' nonverbal communications mean by watching them in various situations and analyzing them later. In romantic relationships, the dating process gives us wonderful opportunities to collect and analyze these nonverbal clues, because we are almost always seeing each other in new situations.

Think back to your first few dates with your partner. Remember how you absorbed every detail of your time together? You paid attention to eye contact, to the play of expression on his or her face, to the tone of voice, the choice of words, the flow of conversation, and the feel of the silences between the two of you. You watched how he treated the waiter at the restaurant, how she reacted to the poignant climax of the movie. And later, after you got home, you replayed the entire date over and over in your mind, looking for clues as to how the other person felt, what the other person meant, why the other person reacted in that particular way. Maybe you even talked with a close friend about the date, looking for a different perspective and further insight into these nuances.

Every subsequent date adds to your stockpile of information and understanding. The next time you go to a restaurant, you compare the way he treats this waitress with the way he treated the last waiter. You watch how she reacts to the violence in this movie and compare it with her reaction to the love scene in the last movie. If you do something completely different—say, a trip to the zoo—the way he reacts to the lions might remind you of the way he grips the steering wheel when he drives, and the rapt expression on her face as she watches the monkeys might be the same expression you saw when she tried escargot for the first time. Seeing these nonverbal clues in different situations helps us gauge what's going on in another person's mind; the more experience we have with this person and his or her nonverbal communication, the better we become at "reading" this person. This is communication at a level beyond words, as it should be. This is bonding.

Each Birth Order Personality has its own set of favorite nonverbal communication techniques:

♦ Onlies scan their environments, looking briefly at everything around them; they are open and expressive with their gestures. When they look at other people, they often imagine what the other is thinking and feeling. Onlies like to watch people at the mall, the airport or other public places and make up little stories about the strangers they see.

♦ First Borns focus on others' faces, looking for hints as to what the other person thinks and feels. They tend to nod often when others are talking and use verbal "coaxers," such as "mm-hmm," to encourage the speaker to continue.

♦ Second Borns concentrate on one item at a time, looking and listening for flaws and thinking about how to improve or change things. In critical mode, they tend to lean back and cross their arms over their chests.

♦ Third Borns scan their environments in the way Onlies do, but they do it more slowly and they are more apt to go back and look at something a second time in order to make comparisons. They tend

to fidget when they get bored; sometimes, they fidget in antici-
pation of becoming bored.

◆ Fourth Borns make more use of peripheral vision than any of the
other birth orders; they cast sidelong glances to see what's going on
around them so they won't be trapped. They pay close attention to
the nonverbal cues others send out; this helps them analyze
other people.

EXERCISE: You can get a glimpse of how other birth order personalities
view the world by imitating their eye movements. After doing this exercise, you'll have a better idea of what others see when you notice these
eye movements in others. You also might become more aware of what
you tend to do with your eyes!

To see what an Only sees: Scan your surroundings. Look at everything around you, but don't linger on anything; just be sure to take in
everything. If you're indoors, see the furniture, decorations, light fixtures,
appliances, windows and whatever you see through the windows. If
you're outdoors, note any other people around, trees and plants, power
lines, areas of sun and shadow.

To see what a First Born sees: Study people's faces. Try to read what
they are thinking, what they are feeling, and what they are likely to do.
Notice the tilt of the head, the mouth, and the lines in the forehead and
around the eyes. When the other person's hand goes to his or her face,
pay attention to what the hand does. Listen to the tone of the other person's voice and try to determine the hidden meaning behind the words.

To see what a Second Born sees: Focus on one thing. Study it in
detail, see the flaws in it, and think about the changes you would make
to improve it. Concentrate on this object; don't look away until you have
thoroughly examined it.

To see what a Third Born sees: Scan your surroundings like the
Only Child does, but do it more slowly. Compare the things you see;
notice how they are alike and how they are different. Go back to objects
or people you have already looked at to compare them with other
objects or people. See if your comparison-looking sparks any new ideas.

To see what a Fourth Born sees: Without turning your head, glance to each side as far as you can. Imagine that someone is sneaking up on you, and you want to be aware of it without letting that person know you are aware. After you check your peripheral vision, go back to looking at whatever is in front of you. If you turn your head to look at something else, check your peripheral vision again.

Nurture Your Bond

Many couples neglect their bond once it is forged. We tend to rely on that first spark to light the fire, and then we figure those first promising flames will burn forever. But the fact is that every lasting relationship, like every good fire, requires careful tending to survive and flourish.

How often have you heard couples or longtime friends say they've "grown apart" over time? It does happen. Distance separates us from our friends and families as we choose different educational or vocational paths. We don't see the same people every day, and even in this age of email and cellular phones, we don't spend time together and usually don't communicate as often as we did when we were just down the street or across town from each other. Sooner or later, we find we don't have much in common anymore with our onetime closest friends, and we make less and less of an effort to keep in touch. Eventually we get down to only exchanging Christmas cards, and after a few years even those may peter out.

The same thing happens with romantic relationships. Without initial bonding and bonding maintenance, the connection between the most united of soul mates eventually will wither and die.

This is why married couples and those in other permanent, committed relationships should date all their lives. It doesn't have to be fancy. Just get out of the house together. Take a walk. Tour a museum. Go to church. Visit friends. Attend a play or a concert. Go shopping just for the heck of it, or take a trip some place neither of you have been before. Do whatever you like, but do it away from home. The more varied your activities, the better, because you get to know each other best as you experience each other in novel settings and situations.

Figuring out what to do on dates with your partner can be challenging, even frustrating, because the five birth order personalities have widely differing reactions to the question, "What do you want to do?" Onlies like to be organized, but they don't like to plan too far in advance. First Borns tend to go along with whatever their partners suggest. Second Borns will raise objections in the form of criticism, whatever is suggested—that fancy restaurant is too expensive, or the movie will be too crowded. Third Borns want to avoid a commitment that might turn out to be boring. Fourth Borns often aren't convinced their partners really want to do things with them.

You also should build some time apart from each other into your schedule. Part of bonding is thinking about the other person when he or she is away; we use this time to analyze and digest the discoveries we made about each other during our last activity together. But this necessary separateness can be difficult for some birth order personalities to accept or enjoy. Onlies excel at "alone time," but Third Borns tend to dislike being alone; they fear becoming bored, which is really loneliness for Third Borns. Fourth Borns often are unable to enjoy alone time because it can make them feel unwanted. Second Borns may feel that their partners want to be alone because the Second Born isn't good enough. First Borns may feel guilty, thinking they've done something to offend their partners.

EXERCISE: One of the toughest questions for any couple to answer is, "What do you want to do tonight?" This exercise serves three purposes: It counters the natural obstacles each Birth Order Personality will put forward in deciding what activity to do; it builds variety into your activities, which gives you and your partner more opportunities to learn about each other; finally, it gives each partner permission to go off and do things on his or her own, also a key element in bonding. Sample lists for a fictional couple named Dan and Karen are at the end of the instructions.

Step 1: Make a list of all the activities you can think of for a date. You can do this with your partner, or you and your partner can make separate lists. No activity is off-limits in this exercise—everything you can think of goes on the list.

Step 2: After you've compiled your list, go through the activities again, but this time put the letter A, B, or C next to each one. (If you and your partner have made separate lists, mark your own lists and then trade lists.) "A" activities are the ones you would enjoy doing. "B" activities are ones you are willing to do because your partner enjoys them. "C" activities are ones that would be an ordeal for you. For example, you might really enjoy a night at the symphony and would put an "A" next to that item, while your partner simply can't see the point of getting all dressed up to listen to 300-year-old music and would mark that activity with a forceful "C." On the other hand, if your partner loves to fish, and you don't mind tagging along as long as you can bring a good book with you, that activity would rate a "B" from you.

Step 3: Put all the "A" and "B" activities for you and your partner on a new list. When you plan a date, take turns choosing an activity from this list. There are two advantages to this: You don't have to wrack your brain deciding what to do, and, since you've already identified the activities you're willing to do either for your own enjoyment or for your partner's, there's no more arguing over what to do. Cross off each activity as you do it; this will help you avoid repetition and falling into the same old dating routine.

Step 4: Make a separate list of the activities you labeled "C," then do the same for the activities your partner labeled "C." These are the things the two of you should do on your own or with friends or family members who would enjoy them. Remember, an important part of bonding is spending time away from your partner. The "C" list gives you and your partner permission to do the things each of you likes to do without feeling guilty for not including the other; at the same time, neither partner needs to feel guilty about not wanting to participate.

Step 5: Update your lists often—every month, for example, or every time you think of something you'd like to do.

Sample lists for Dan and Karen

Things to do on a date:
Go for a walk
Shop for a new stereo
Fly a kite
Wash the car
Go hunting
See a play
Go to a concert
Attend the fair
Go horseback riding
Go out for ice cream
See a movie
Go to dinner with friends
Go skydiving
Have a picnic
Go to the beach
Drive around and look for garage sales
Play volleyball

Dan's ratings:
Go for a walk—B
Shop for a new stereo—A
Fly a kite—A
Wash the car—A
Go hunting—A
See a play—B
Go to a concert—C
Attend the fair—C
Go horseback riding—A

Go out for ice cream—B
See a movie—A
Go to dinner with friends—A
Go skydiving—C
Have a picnic—B
Go to the beach—A
Drive around and look for garage sales—C
Play volleyball—A

Karen's ratings:
Go for a walk—A
Shop for a new stereo—C
Fly a kite—B
Wash the car—B
Go hunting—C
See a play—A
Go to a concert—A
Attend the fair—C
Go horseback riding—A
Go out for ice cream—A
See a movie—B
Go to dinner with friendsA
Go skydiving—A
Have a picnic—A
Go to the beach—A
Drive around and look for garage sales—A
Play volleyball—C

Things to do on a date for Dan and Karen
Go for a walk (Dan B, Karen A)
Fly a kite (Dan A, Karen B)
Wash the car (Dan A, Karen B)
See a play (Dan B, Karen A)
Go horseback riding (Dan A, Karen A)

Go out for ice cream (Dan B, Karen A)
See a movie (Dan A, Karen B)
Go to dinner with friends (Dan A, Karen A)
Have a picnic (Dan B, Karen A)
Go to the beach (Dan A, Karen A)

Things that are OK for Dan to do
without Karen
Shop for a new stereo
Go hunting
Play volleyball

Things that are OK for Karen to do
without Dan
Go to a concert
Go skydiving
Drive around and look for garage sales

Create a Loving Atmosphere

Unless you and your partner spend most of your time dating or going off on your own, you'll spend a lot of time at home with each other. For some of us, "home" has a negative connotation; as children, home was where we had chores to do, where we got punished, where we fought with our siblings or where we listened to our parents fight. The fun part of our childhood was away from home—at the park or playground, at a friend's house, at the mall. As adults, we may carry the same associations into our own homes. Onlies may feel like a heavy weight settles on their shoulders when they cross the threshold and lifts when they leave home. First Borns may feel like they have to walk on eggshells at home to avoid offending their partners. Second Borns may feel exceptionally sensitive to anger at home. Third Borns may feel that they have to carry the heaviest load at home. Fourth Borns may feel that they don't really belong and aren't really wanted at home.

The things we say to each other—or, more precisely, how we say those things—can exacerbate or ease those negative feelings. If we make negative comments, our partners' negative feelings become stronger, and vice versa. When our partners say things like, "I hate the way that scraggly rose bush looks in front of the house," or, "This couch is the most uncomfortable thing I've ever sat on," we tend to feel like we're the ones who caused these reactions, rather than the rose bush and the couch.

We create an atmosphere for ourselves and other people by what we say and how we say it. If you say to your partner as he or she opens the oven, "I love the smell of bread baking," your partner will feel an atmosphere of love. If you say, "Boy, I hate the smell of burnt cookies," your partner will feel an atmosphere of hate.

It sounds too simple to be true, doesn't it? But it really does work, and it works on almost any scale. When Jimmy Carter told us in the 1970s that the United States was suffering from a "great malaise," Americans felt depressed, individually and collectively. But when John F. Kennedy challenged the country to put a man on the moon, Americans felt energized and confident. What these two presidents said and how they said it acted as subliminal cues for their audiences, who responded to these cues in kind.

The Reverend Phil Webb, a pastor in an Iowa church, had a gift for creating an atmosphere of love and harmony in his congregation. He did this by regularly introducing portions of the service with the words "I love this passage," or "I love this song." This continual reinforcement, albeit on a subconscious level, encouraged members of the congregation to respond in loving ways. And while we cannot always quantify the results of such reinforcement, the Reverend Webb's congregation provided a remarkable measurement of the atmosphere he created: When an expensive remodeling project for the church came before the congregation for a vote, the members approved it by ninety-three percent.

The five birth order personalities have their own ways of making positive and negative statements. Onlies are most likely to say they "love" or "hate" things, because in their imaginary worlds even inanimate objects have human characteristics. Onlies love things and situations that make them feel organized. They hate things and situations that make them feel disorganized or pressured. When an Only says he hates something, it's really an expression of frustration.

First Borns are least likely to say they love or hate something; their strategy is to avoid making such strong statements that might offend others. Instead, First Borns will gently agree or (less commonly) disagree with such statements made by others. If an Only asks a First Born, "Don't you just love roller coasters?" the First Born is likely to respond with something like, "They're OK, I guess," which can be taken as agreement or disagreement but doesn't commit the First Born to anything.

Instead of using "love" and "hate," Second Borns are more likely to offer tempered compliments or criticism. The Second Born response to the Only's question about roller coasters might be something like, "I'd like them better if they had more comfortable restraints for the seats." Even when they say they "love" something, Second Borns are likely to include a criticism of that thing in the same breath.

Third Borns tend to use "like" instead of love, which may be a reflection of their attempts to avoid boredom. "Like" implies that something is OK for now, but it doesn't carry the same level of commitment as "love." If a Third Born says he "loves" roller coasters, others might expect him to ride on one at every opportunity. But if the Third Born only admits he "likes" roller coasters, he won't feel obligated to ride one the next time he goes to an amusement park.

Fourth Borns tend to make a lot of "hate" statements and few "love" statements because they try to communicate their maturity by talking about how hard they work. This often translates into a pattern of complaining; a Fourth Born talking about roller coasters might say, "The last time I went on a rollercoaster, I stood in line for an hour in 90-degree weather." You have to ask the Fourth Born whether the ride was worth the wait to find out how he or she feels about roller coasters.

Choosing our words with an ear tuned to hearing the difference between positive and negative is a simple way to influence the atmosphere in our homes, our work places or anywhere else. It can make an incredible difference in how people around you feel, and, consequently, how they react to you. But it's something many of us overlook in the rush and bustle of modern life.

EXERCISE: Look for opportunities to make positive comments, even when things don't seem so positive. If you've had a bad day at work, for example, greet your partner with, "Boy, am I glad to be home!" instead of "Boy, did I have a rotten day!" You can describe your bad day later, but your first statement makes it clear that your negative feelings are not associated with your partner.

When your partner makes negative statements, try these responses to better understand the real message your partner is trying to convey.

- If your partner is an Only: When he or she says, "I hate …," respond with, "You sound frustrated."
- If your partner is a First Born: When he or she says, "I guess that's OK," respond with, "You may not agree, but …"
- If your partner is a Second Born: When he or she says some variation of, "OK, but …," respond with, "It may not be perfect, but …"
- If your partner is a Third Born: When he or she says some variation of, "Not really," respond with, "It's OK if you don't like this."
- If your partner is a Fourth Born: When he or she complains, respond with, "You've done a lot of (thinking about/work on) this, haven't you?"

Adjust Your Thinking
We may have challenged your thinking with our ideas here. That's OK; in fact, that's one of the things we set out to do. Thinking really is nothing more than putting order to chaos. As soon as we're born, we are surrounded by chaos, and we begin thinking to sort and organize the chaos, to put it in order. Of course, we can't possibly get everything in

order, so some chaos remains; therefore, we keep thinking. Accepting new ideas requires us to invite chaos into our ordered world and then organize and sort the new idea. That's what we've done with this new concept of birth order. The study of personality always has been chaotic because there has been no real order to it. Our birth order gives order to the world of personality.

Of course, your reaction to the information we've presented here can be influenced by birth order. If you're an Only, you may be inclined to reject it because accepting new ideas means reorganizing your views of the world. If you're a First Born, you may look around for more information about birth order to feed your research-hungry mind. If you're a Second Born, you might be inclined to test birth order among your friends and relatives to look for mistakes in our descriptions. If you're a Third Born, you might find yourself comparing the information here with other works on relationships or birth order. And if you're a Fourth Born, you may find yourself using this information to help you analyze the people around you.

One thing we're sure of: If you make use of the information we've given you, you'll find that you'll have a better understanding of yourself and your partner. You might even find yourself looking at your friends and colleagues with a view to determining their birth order, and if you do that, you'll have a better understanding of them, too.

Don't be surprised if you find yourself re-reading a particular section—or two or three—of this book. There's a lot to absorb, especially if you weren't familiar with this new birth order when you started. It might take a while before linking birth order and behavior comes easily, and that's OK. This information is meant to help for a lifetime, and a refresher never hurts. Even the exercises are designed so that you can use them as often as you want to.

And, speaking of exercises, we have one last one for you to measure what you and your partner have learned about each other's Birth Order Personality. In this exercise, you are going to describe your partner's personality, and your partner is going to describe yours. When each description is finished, the person being described will let the other know how he or she has done. Give honest feedback to each other; this is not the time to let your partner think he or she understands you if he or she doesn't, and vice versa.

To explain each other's personality, describe the following characteristics:

- How your partner's Birth Order Personality developed
- Your partner's thinking pattern
- Your partner's way of dealing with emotions
- You partner's way of expressing love, according to birth order
- Your partner's communication pattern
- What your partner needs from other people
- What causes your partner to feel good
- What you enjoy about your partner's characteristics

Don't panic if you don't hit it exactly on the nose right away. It takes practice to think about birth order and its effects this way. This exercise, like all the others we've provided, is meant to help you learn about each other and understand each other. If you misread or misinterpret things here and there, all that means is that you have another opportunity to learn. And that is the hallmark of a healthy, fulfilling relationship.

Acknowledgments

As in any endeavor, many, many people had a hand in creating this book. We extend our appreciation first to Alfred Adler, who began the quest to understand human personalities and behaviors through birth order; to Dr. Taibi Kahler, whose work with life mini-scripts helped inspire Cliff's discoveries about birth order personalities; and to the thousands of clients whose openness about themselves and their lives continue to illuminate the myriad intricacies of birth order.

Exploring birth order is a continual learning curve, and we thank those readers, students, and researchers whose questions and life stories have given us additional insight into birth order. These curious minds will further refine the study of Birth Order Personality; we can't wait to learn what they will teach us.

Our agent, Barbara Doyen, is tireless in her dedication, skillful and talented in her work, and contagious in her enthusiasm. Thank you for bringing us together, and remember that we like you because you're you.

Paula Munier, our editor at Fair Winds, has earned our respect and trust as sincere cheerleader and constructive critic. Thank you for taking a good project and making it better, and thank you for your encouragement and advocacy in the process.

Most important, thanks to our families for their patience and support: Kathy Isaacson and Bud Schmunk, who forgave us for the long hours we spent on the phone or the computer and away from them; our children, Duane, Mary, Shirley, Linda, Kevin and Christopher, who will never know how much they taught us; Clyde and Virginia, who bragged about their daughter-in-law before there was a reason to; and Dick and Jan, who believed in the possibilities down the road less traveled. We don't even want to imagine where we would be without you.

About the Authors

Cliff Isaacson is the author of five books, four of them about birth order, and founder of the Upper Des Moines Counseling Center in Algona, Iowa, where he continues his counseling practice. His birth order discoveries have helped thousands of people better understand themselves by showing how everyone's ideas of love, self-worth, justice and communication vary according to his or her Birth Order Personality.

Isaacson is a United Methodist minister, a Diplomate member of the American Psychotherapy Association, and a member of Mensa. He is the father of five grown children and lives in northwest Iowa with his wife, Kathy.

Meg Schneider is an award-winning writer and journalist with more than a decade of experience in television, radio and print media. Thanks to her staunch belief in lifelong learning and an aversion to well-trodden paths, she also has been at various times a restaurateur, a business manager, a veterinary assistant, an advertising saleswoman, and an air traffic control trainee. Originally from Iowa, she now lives in Central New York with her husband Bud, honorary sons Chris and Justin, and three dogs.